Cross-Cultural Orientation Programs

Cross-Cultural

GARDNER PRESS, INC.
NEW YORK

Distributed by Halsted Press
Division of John Wiley & Sons, Inc.

Richard W. Brislin

East-West Center

Paul Pedersen

University of Minnesota

Orientation Programs

GARDNER PRESS, INC.
32 Washington Square West
New York, New York 10011

Distributed solely by the HALSTED PRESS Division of John Wiley & Sons, Inc., New York

Library of Congress Cataloging in Publication Data

Brislin, Richard W 1945–
   Cross-cultural orientation programs.

   Includes bibliographical references and index.
   1. Intercultural education. I. Pedersen, Paul,
1936– joint author.   II. Title.
LC1099.B74   370.19′6   75–41358
ISBN 0–470–14993–0

Printed in the United States of America
1   2   3   4   5   6   7   8   9

PREFACE

As we write, we have a picture in our minds of you, the reader, as a person looking for orientation methods designed to improve relationships among people from various cultures. We are assuming that readers want to reach beyond their own allegiance to national, racial, ethnic, or life-style values. To do that they need to know what others are doing to bridge cultural differences and to bring persons from various backgrounds together in a shared learning experience. Cultures, like walls, establish boundaries, protect us from our enemies, keep others out and sometimes keep ourselves in. Also, like walls, cultures have gates that can be opened, letting us come and go freely. Unlike walls, none of us owns the cultural fence. Nobody controls the gate that allows free access to those who know where to find it and who have the adventurous spirit to enter.

Why should different people be interested in one another? Why should harmony and cooperation not come naturally between reasonable adults? We are making several assumptions about intercultural contact. First, there is the idea that more knowledge about others different from ourselves helps us to see ourselves as others see us, rather than assuming that others see us as we see ourselves, or depending entirely on a "self reference criterion". If we can have more contact with outsiders, we might become more tolerant and able to understand their point of view. In order to result in harmony, however, the contact must be made under "favorable" conditions and not—as is more typically the case—under unfavorable conditions, which are more likely to result in hostility. Contact with other cultures is not *by itself* likely to bring about harmony without careful planning (Amir, 1969).

Second, we are being forced to work with other cultures, whether we like it or not. In recent years our schools have been desegrated and integrated by law; occupations have been opened that heretofore excluded applicants on the basis of race and sex; our larger corporations have assumed multinational influence; political disputes in any other part of the world are likely to disrupt our own daily routine back home. We are no longer free to isolate ourselves from other countries around the world or other cultures in our own neighborhood. We are being forced to choose whether to integrate with them, be assimilated by them, or otherwise accommodate ourselves to other points of view. The only choice we have is the *mode* of our interaction—whether by force, conflict, and war on the one hand or through peaceful coexistence on the other.

Third, we can learn much about ourselves from other people who see us differently than we see ourselves. People are different both individually and collectively as persons and as groups in ways that affect their attitudes toward one another. We have learned one way of looking at the world and behave according to how we perceive the world, but other people see the same world differently and therefore behave differently. No two persons see the world in exactly the same way, and the more different their experiences, the more likely their perceptions are to conflict. A group or culture includes persons who more or less agree in their perception, giving them a shared identity. The more similar their perception, the more likely they are to agree. Each of us belongs to many such groups, and, as our experiences influence us, we change from one group to another. The point is, if we talk only with persons who agree with us, we will become locked into one, but not the only one, way of seeing the world around us.

Getting together with persons from other cultures can indeed be dangerous, as xenophobic isolationists are quick to point out. First, it is true that diversity can create disunity and cause trouble, especially for people who believe that in a strong society everybody believes the same things. Some may see us moving toward some single truth where the differences of ethnicity, religion, and race are an embarrassment, reminding us of our primitive past. Back when integration was the goal of the civil rights movement and when the melting pot was proof of America's success, we tried to eliminate cultural differences. But we found that we could not destroy our differences without destroying ourselves in the process. Our national motto, *E Pluribus Unum*, suggests that our source of strength is not in our sameness but, in fact, in our plurality!

A second danger is illustrated in the argument that treating persons differently because of their race, religion, nationality, or sex is itself a sign of prejudice. We are caught in a dilemna. Differences are dangerous when they result in one group looking down on another, but those same differences can be a valuable resource in a "mutualistic" relationship in which we trade off our differences in a harmonious exchange with one another.

When we emphasize our differences, because of what we believe or because I was born here and you were born there, we are confronting a third danger of cultural differences. People begin to choose up sides according to skin color, culture, or sex and forget about our interdependence on one another. As a society we become fragmented by dissention, disagreement, and bickering, while individuals are torn apart having to choose where they belong. This could be avoided by building on our similarities and the goals we share with others so that we can work together more effectively. Harmony does not necessarily mean everyone agreeing with everyone else, but rather a process of adjustment in which we learn to adjust our lives and, in some cases, agree to disagree. Some persons can never discuss a controversy without trying to bring the other person around to their point of view and to analyze every disagreement in terms of "winners" or "losers" (White, 1969). To "lose" an argument is to fail to convince the other person that we are right and they are wrong; in fact, both of us may disagree without *necessarily* one being right and the other wrong. Even flexibility and broadmindedness can become a new kind of intolerant conformity prejudiced against the "red-necked racist" for what he believes. A sensitivity training group of university students might pride themselves in being liberal, open, flexible, and accepting to the point that they could become enraged with anger describing the stupidity and rigidity of critics! We exclude others from our group some-times for the very reason that they have attempted to exclude us!

The first section of this book is intended to introduce many of the concepts essential to training designs covered in the later chapters. Cross-cultural orientation requires a rigorous rationale, and some specific criteria for evaluating a training design are described which begin to examine the central issue of whether training should be general or specific. The resistance to training is also discussed. Some persons prefer their own point of view regardless of cultural context. Others prefer to let sojourners learn on their own, without any preparation, through the shock of cultural conflicts resulting from their own mistakes. Intercultural training has been surprisingly unpopular in the preparation of technical assistants for assignment in other cultures, requiring some explanation and interpretation of the scanty data available to us. Finally, there is a discussion of whether inter-cultural training has a future. The authors are commit-ted to the view that intercultural training is essential to har-monious intercultural contact.

In the second chapter we review the many published accounts of the *content* found in various cross-cultural train-ing programs. Drawing from the extremely diverse litera-ture, much of which is available only in limited-distribution technical reports otherwise known as "fugitive materials," we have tried to highlight what we think is especially good and what we feel could have applicability in various programs designed to achieve various goals. We have drawn from many types of organizations that have been involved in crosscultural training, including the Peace Corps, the military, business, industry, colleges and universities, state-wide boards of education, and mental health agencies. Readers will probably be selective in the use of this chapter, drawing one idea here, another there, for use in programs they design themselves. The fifth chapter, in part, describes how this eclectic procedure, based on fitting program elements to program goals, might occur.

In choosing material to be reviewed in the second chapter, we have had to depend on programs that are described in write-ups of some kind, either in the published literature, or in the "mimeographed press," that is, fugitive descriptions that we have been able to collect. In some cases, for reasons of space, a program is not included because it bears great similarity to another described herein. For instance, Brislin (1970) reviewed the United States Navy's personal response program for training Marines about to be stationed overseas, but since it incorporates elements found in other programs (e.g., role-playing, guided reading, action recommendations) reviewed here, we did not include it in this book.

The third chapter contains descriptions of various audiences we feel might be the target of various cross-cultural training programs. The classic audience has been people about to live for a significantly long period of time in a culture other than their own. Although this audience will continue to receive a great deal of attention, other groups are increasingly receiving (and many times requesting) orientation programs that will help them understand people from various cultures or subcultures. Some potential audiences are to be found very close to home rather than in far-off distant lands. These include mental health workers, sophisticated tourists who want more than the cliche of 14 day–15 country packaged tours, and various organizations who are being challenged by the recent values grouped under the term "sexism." Recent conferences involving professionals from all three of these areas, although not using the language of cross-cultural training and orientation employed throughout this book, have made recommendations for the type of training we outline here.

The fourth chapter covers program evaluation, a topic rarely covered in descriptions and discussions of cross-cultural training. We attempt to explain the reasons for the previous neglect, and this treatment includes an analysis of the conflicting pressures of hard-nosed evaluation and subjective experience that face the organizers of cross-cultural training programs. Research designs are suggested whose principles should be both flexible in application and strong in providing analysis of what is good and what is bad about a program. The fifth chapter contains guidelines on the planning details of organizing a program. The main point is that the provision of food, transportation, and other seemingly trivial details have to take a place alongside goals of cross-cultural understanding and training methods, or else success in the latter will not occur. The practical guidelines are based largely on our own experience of organizing training programs and coping with such problems as a guest speaker not showing up and our having no fast substitute ready and waiting, or serving meat to a vegetarian audience. We hope this final chapter will show how the ideas in the first four chapters can be put into practice.

As you read about the various aspects of cross-cultural orientation programs, you might share some of our enthusiasm for the process of intercultural training. Cultural differences are too frequently seen as a barrier or problem and too seldom recognized as a resource for learning. As our society becomes more sensitized to the importance of cultural identity, one would hope that the whole field of cross-cultural training might disappear and be swallowed up as an essential aspect of all educational opportunities to which people are exposed.

The authors would like to thank the following people for their help at various stages of the preparation of this manuscript: Ann Brislin, Joy Ichiyama, Patricia Kim, Joy Norton, Karen Shiroma, Hazel Tatsuno, and William Weeks. During the final writing of the manuscript, the second author was a senior fellow at the Culture Learning Institute, East-West Center. Both authors would like to thank administrators of the Center for the atmosphere and stimulation which made the book possible.

Richard W. Brislin
Paul Pederson

Honolulu, Hawaii
Minneapolis, Minnesota

September 1975

Contents

CHAPTER 1

INTRODUCTION

The terms *cross-cultural orientation programs* and *cross-cultural education* are sometimes confused. Cross-cultural orientation programs are designed to teach members of one culture ways of interacting effectively, with minimal interpersonal misunderstanding, in another culture. They are usually short-term programs: the vast majority are less than 2 weeks long, and some occur over a period of approximately 4 hours. Cross-cultural education, on the other hand, refers to the total set of experiences people might have when studying in a country other than the one they consider their home country. Cross-cultural education also refers to long-term (i.e., 2 to 4 years, or the time needed to obtain a college degree) programs that have an international scope to them. Cross-cultural orientation programs can be an extremely useful part of a longer term cross-cultural educational experience, since they can introduce the longer experience and prepare people so that they might obtain maximal benefit from the long-term program. In addition to the field of education, however, cross-cultural orientation programs can be beneficial to many audiences,

1

because there is an increasing amount of contact between people from different cultural backgrounds in numerous areas within modern-day society. Examples include multinational corporations, governmental agencies, bilingual education programs within a given country, and international tourism. We cover the various areas in which cross-cultural orientation programs might have an impact in our chapter on "audiences."

Desirable Aspects of Cross-Cultural Training Programs

The primary purpose of cross-cultural orientations is to encourage constructive and nonstressful interaction between members of different cultures. Of course, such interaction should occur immediately after training as well as months after training has been completed. From our review of existing programs as well as our experience in this area we feel that the following list of desirable aspects is necessary if an orientation program is to be effective. In this list it is assumed that a program is being designed for individuals from one culture who (for any number of reasons) are about to live in another culture.

1. Assumptions should be tested by empirical data. That is, research data should be brought to bear on a program's methods and goals. Several programs proceed on the assumption that inducing self-awareness of people's own prejudices and basic values should help them understand and interact effectively with others. There is, however, no evidence that people high in self-awareness interact with others more effectively than people low in self-awareness. This problem is central in the culture-general versus culture-specific controversy (to be covered below), because self-awareness training is part of culture-general programs.

2. A reasonable set of training goals should be established. Such goals should also be capable of being researched, that is, should be subjected to study so that they can be modified or eliminated if necessary. For obvious reasons the military has had more access to resources for researching training goals than most other sectors of society. Spector's (1969, pp. 8–12)

list of goals for the Troop-Community Relations Program in Korea is very reasonable and can provide guidelines for other programs.

- a. Develop in Americans positive regard for host nationals.
- b. Develop an understanding of the fundamental similarities among human beings.
- c. Develop habits of dealing with each host national on an individual rather than a stereotyped level.
- d. Provide trainee "with a way of observing, analyzing, and integrating cross-cultural phenomena which permits him to deal independently and realistically with the situations and problems that he encounters while living abroad."
- e. Prepare trainees to withstand culture shock.
- f. Develop feelings of responsibility in each person for the improvement of relationships with host nationals.
- g. Reinforce training "through group facilitation and support, and . . . develop within each individual a sense of group involvement."
- h. Give specific information about host-national attitudes, customs, and the like.

Another set of goals was gathered from the writings of several researchers. The amount of agreement regarding goals was substantial (Guthrie, 1966, 1975; Jordan, 1966; Grace and Hofland, 1967; Loubert, 1967; Eachus, 1968; Wedge et al., 1968; Bass, 1969, Triandis, 1975). Their goals include attempts to:

- a. Improve awareness of customs and interpersonal skills, including techniques for dealing with culture shock phenomena.
- b. Help the student develop basic communication skills by teaching key phrases in the foreign language and techniques for speaking through interpreters.
- c. Impart knowledge about the foreign culture, complete with practical skills and know-how needed to get along satisfactorily in the culture.
- d. Attempt to impart sensitivity to others, reducing prejudice and inducing respect, even toward those for-

eign cultural values and practices that make little
sense to the student.

    e. Attempt to induce enthusiasm for the job.

    f. Provide opportunities to maintain skills during peri-
ods of absence from other cultures.

    g. Above all, emphasize honesty in relations with others.

    3. Provide transition from the training setting to the
real world. This point simply says that people should not be
favorable toward foreign nationals only during, for instance,
in a short-term program, their 4-hour training session, but
also during work hours and free time. Techniques must be
devised to *transfer* the favorable behaviors learned during
training to the real world. This point brings up what has
been called the "Lena Horne-Harry Belefonte" problem.
People sometimes interact with out-group[1] members as
handsome as these two entertainers, and grow to like them.
But there is no *transfer* from these handsome people to average out-group members.

    4. Provide social support for favorable behavior to host
nationals. This point emphasizes that there is a difference between the individual in training and the same individual in his
social setting outside of training. The effects of a good training
program can be undone by the pressure of an individual's
peers. For instance, an individual might want to make friends
with a host national (remembering his training), but his cyni-
cal, prejudiced peers may ridicule this "unnatural" desire. The
spirit of the training must be widespread and not limited to
only the 4-hour session during which trainees participated in
the cross-cultural orientation. There must be widespread social
support for the behavior recommended in training. One of
Spector's (1969) goals, mentioned above (point 2g) is to provide
this social support. Note that when all people in a group are
practicing the range of behaviors recommended in training,
there are many models available for any one individual to
imitate. Guthrie (1969) and David (1972) feel that such modell-
ing and imitation of favorable behaviors are essential to program effectiveness.

    Rewards and recognition, related to the above points,

---

[1]An out-group is a group to which a given person does not belong, that is, is not
a member.

should be available to those people who perform well in the area of cross-cultural interaction. Recent research (Vroom, 1964; Graen, 1969; Mitchell and Biglan, 1971) has shown that workers perform effectively when they see their behavior as instrumental in gaining rewards. That is, workers are effective when they see a link between their behavior and desired rewards. Some people who might benefit from cross-cultural training do not work effectively at their job because they see no rewards for behavior recommended in the training. If cross-cultural training is to be effective, rewards (promotions, commendations, etc.) must be available for those people who engage in exemplary cross-cultural interactions. The rewards must be as frequent as those given to people who are successful at other aspects of their job, such as skill in the technical task assigned to them. Even social and behavioral scientists who shun the approach of behaviorism agree that people migrate toward those aspects of a situation that obviously yield rewards. If technical skill rather than effective cross-cultural interaction is seen to yield the bigger rewards in terms of, for instance, salary increases and promotions, then people will put their effort into technical skills.

5. Provide opportunities for evaluating the effectiveness of training, especially the long-range effects of behavior after training. This point is elaborated on later in a major section devoted to the evaluation problem.

6. Replicate major findings. The basis of knowledge is that facts manifest themselves again and again under the scrutiny of different people. If one researcher or administrator discovers a principle of cross-cultural training, another should try to replicate it.

7. Provide follow-up training. In addition to sessions before assignment to a specific post-training position, trainees should have additional training during any assignment that involves interaction with people from other cultures. These additional sessions may provide reinforcement for original learning and can provide the opportunity to discuss specific problems encountered during overseas duty.

These seven points are summarized in Table 1, and are listed as desirable aspects to be considered before, during, and after training.

Table 1
Desirable Aspects of Cross-Cultural Training Programs

TIME

Before Training	During Training	After Training
Gather data on assumptions	Provide transfer from training to real world	Evaluate effectiveness
Set up reasonable goals	Provide social support to individuals	Replicate major findings
		Provide follow-up training

Culture-General Versus Culture-Specific Controversy

Any person who makes decisions about the content of a cross-cultural orientation program will have to address a dichotomy that has divided practitioners. A lively debate has centered around the issue of whether training should be culture-specific or general. General training refers to such topics as self-awareness and sensitivity training that allow one to learn about himself as preparation for interaction in *any* culture. Specific training refers to information about a given culture and guidelines for interaction with members of that culture. For instance, eating habits, religious customs, etiquette in interpersonal interactions, and decision-making styles might be taught. Unfortunately, the debate has centered on opinion and educated comment, because there are so few facts known. Most agree, however, that culture-general training is often necessary because some people (in the military, industry, academia) are not assigned to a specific country until the last minute, or because some programs have participants about to depart for a variety of countries. Because the issue has generated a certain amount of "heat" (we have witnessed rather loud discussions of the issues at professional meetings), we cite people's writings verbatim so as to minimize possible misinterpretation.

Proponents of culture-general training include Stewart, Danielian, and Foster (1969) who developed the Contrast-American technique. They wrote:

> . . . it is *insight* into one's own values and assumptions
> that permits the growth of a perspective which recognizes
> that differing sets of values and assumptions exist (i.e., cultural
> relativism), and development of the potential for greater un-
> derstanding of another culture (p. 7).

They then described their technique in which an American
trainee role-plays with a person who manifests values not normally associated with the American stereotype; called the
Contrast American. This latter person is not from any specific
country, but rather represents a composite person quite different than the "average" American.

> The cognitive confrontation brings one's own values and
> assumptions into question, making the trainee more aware of
> the cultural determinant in himself. Self-awareness, in turn,
> results in greater understanding and empathy with the values
> and assumptions of a member of another culture; continuing
> the reciprocal relationship, this increased understanding
> once again yields a deeper cultural self-awareness which in-
> creases other awareness ad infinitum (p. 8).

Stewart et al. (1969) emphasized that this technique
should only be a part of a training program.

Another point of view is that of Roth (1969) who ques-
tioned the utility of cultural general training. He assumed:

> It is not essential that members of different cultures be
> extremely affectionate toward each other—however, it is
> both important and necessary that rational co-operation oc-
> curs between them. Rational co-operation can take place be-
> tween individuals who do not greatly admire or respect each
> other, just as close interpersonal relationships can give rise to
> very irrational and uncooperative behavior. It seems to us,
> then, that training programs must emphasize these rational
> bases for co-ordinating action (p. 4).

He further commented on the notion that a 6-week program (e.g., sensitivity training) can change attitudes. It should
be noted that the actual cross-cultural programs to be re-

viewed most often entail less time than 6 weeks—sometimes only a few hours.

> It may be unreasonable to expect to change a man's beliefs about another nationality in the period of six-weeks of pretraining, when his attitudes and beliefs have taken most of a life-time to form. Therefore, although a research or training program interested in the deep-seated feelings of participants is praiseworthy, it appears to us that given the constraints within which training programs operate and the nature of the interaction settings which are characteristic of many cross-cultural contacts—such emphasis and concern seem unrealistic. To us, then, the basic aim of training for cross-cultural interaction should focus on the conscious and rational level with a relatively short period of time utilizing known and proven pedagogical techniques (pp. 4–5).

In other words, specific methods (e.g., how to make decisions with member of country X) for dealing with specific cultures may be much more valuable than cultural-general training.

Triandis (1968), who has participated in extensive research into cross-cultural training, wrote of his own experience:

> I was born and raised in Greece, but I have lived for more than half of my life in North America. Furthermore, I was exposed to heavy doses of several other cultures in the form of German teachers during my first decade, a French high school during my second decade, and a brief exposure to an Italian high school during the second World War occupation of Greece by the axis forces (pp. 57–58).

He then wrote, cautioning against generalizing from one case:

> In spite of this extensive cross-cultural training, I experienced a mild culture shock in Calcutta, India. The fact that I am fluent in several languages has only helped my adjustment in those cultures where these languages are used.

Outside these cultures there is a sharp drop in comfort. The amount of discomfort is similar to what happens when I visit behind the Iron Curtain—the social system is different and there is too much about it that I do not understand, or like, so I feel uncomfortable. Similarly, when the language is unknown, the unpredictability of the situation is enough to raise my anxiety. I am not at home. A person with much less cross-cultural experience might very well feel much more anxious (p. 58).

Triandis then recommended cross-cultural training for specific competencies.

Our position is that of Roth and Triandis, but no reader should fully accept either the specific or general approach to training without much more data on the question. We hope that future research will focus on this issue. In reviewing actual programs in a later section, such as the work of Triandis and others on the "cultural assimilator," the data supporting the culture-specific view will be reviewed. The small number of existing empirical studies, however, does not justify unqualified acceptance of either view. The most reasonable alternative is to recommend both general and specific training appropriate to a target culture. Future research, however, can be expected to match specific training models with an audience's goals according to their need to know about specific cultures, relationships, and objectives, as analyzed by the trainer. The complexities of each cross-cultural situation prevent simple-solution approaches.

Intercultural Adjustment

The previous sections dealt with qualities of a good program and some basic assumptions about cross-cultural orientations. Cross-cultural training for orientation is most successful when there is a careful analysis of the potential difficulties a group of trainees might have in the future and some understanding of why they might have these difficulties. In a conference on intercultural adjustment, the Group for the Advancement of Psychiatry (1966) credited overseas failure nearly always to personal difficulties, such as the inability to adapt or deal with interpersonal relationships in a foreign situation. This finding suggests much greater emphasis on psychological aspects of the selection and training process, even though there may be much resistance to the use of psychological tests in selection decisions (Harris, 1975). One early psychological study on intercultural adjustment of American university students overseas by Taba (1953) showed that persons with a rigid personality and definite preconceptions about their own culture tend to form attitudes through emotional reactions rather than intellectual analysis. More recent findings (Brein and David, 1971) have confirmed the importance of emotional aspects for intercultural adjustment. Persons who have a more difficult time making an adjustment to another culture have tended to be less flexible in their personality characteristics and have tended to depend on intellectual insights of a rationally ordered existence in defining their attitudes.

The cross-cultural factors that are most troubling are often not the more obvious differences of dress, gestures, or food, although the exotic aspects of these differences are cited to illustrate cultural differences. The adjustment process demands a reordering of daily behavior habits in subtle ways which might escape conscious awareness, such as different uses of the same word, different status symbols that must not be insulted, different traditional values that must be recognized or different views on the importance of personal relationships. These aspects of adjustment conflict with culturally related behavior habits that can be extremely difficult to change.

Triandis (1971) calls attention to the Skaggs–Robinson hypothesis and the Osgood transfer surface which suggest that any new situation (such as another culture) that involves the same stimulus and the same response pattern is least difficult. For example, if we know how to drive a car in one country we might expect little difficulty driving another car in another country. When both the situation and the required response are different, we are confronted with a simple situation of learning without having to "un-learn" any previous response. When we are prompted to behave in a foreign country according to back-home cues we are most likely to encounter trouble. When the same stimulus requires a very different response, we are confronted with a much more difficult situation. If we come across a word in some foreign language or even the same language in a different country (United States or Australia) which is used *like* a completely different word in a person's own language or dialect, there might be some difficulty in reacting to it. For instance, in Australia "spastic" is the common word used for handicapped children, and visitors will see small signs directing them to the "Spastic Children's Center." Australians visiting the U.S. would, in contrast, be shocked to see a sign directing them to the "Crippled Children's Center." In each case the same facility requires a very different label to be both accurate and inoffensive.

Lee (1966) described the unconscious reference to one's own cultural values as the "Self Reference Criterion" held by people of all cultures. We observe others from our own point of view, comparing them with ourselves as the standard of "normal." There are fairly obvious dangers in being tied to our own point of view, and only disciplined effort will extinguish it. Lee (1969) described a Cultural Analysis System with four steps for authenticating cross-cultural communications to minimize this bias. (1) Define the problem or goal in terms of American cultural traits, habits, or norms. (2) Define the problem or goal in terms of the foreign cultural traits, habits, or norms, but do not make any value judgments about it. (3) Isolate the self reference criterion influence on the problem and examine it carefully to see how it might complicate the problem. (4) Redefine the problem without the self reference criterion influence and identify solutions that would optimize goal accomplishment. The culture assimilator (Triandis, 1975) describes a training design, covered in later chapters, to minimize this bias.

Barna (1972) cites five barriers to accurate communications across cultures. First, there is the obvious barrier of language differences. Language is much more than learning new sound symbols. Knowing a little of the foreign language may allow a person only to make a "fluent fool" of himself if he is unaware of the implicit meanings behind those symbols. Second, there are nonverbal communications such as gestures, postures, and other metamessages on which we depend for communications. There is some difficulty in recognizing unspoken codes which come so automatically that they may not even be conscious in our own more familiar culture but which will communicate a definite feeling or attitude. The third barrier of preconceptions and stereotypes are the overgeneralized beliefs that provide structure to the scrambled raw experiences of our own or other cultures. People perceive pretty much what they want to or expect to perceive, screening out many contradictory impressions. When we first become slightly aware of another culture, these half-formed stereotypes are most likely to betray communications. The stereotype has a tendency to become realized through the self-fulfilling prophecy of the communicator. A fourth deterrent is a tendency to evaluate, in an approving or disapproving judgment, to the content of communication received from others. "Everyone speaks with an accent except people who talk like myself." Evaluation frequently interferes with understanding the other person from the other person's point of view and falls into the trap of communicating that "I know better than you what you should do." A fifth barrier is the typically high level of anxiety that shrouds cross-cultural communications, where we are dealing with unfamiliar experiences. This phenomena is dealt with more extensively in the section of this book on culture shock.

We might summarize the problems of learning and teaching about another culture in terms of five separate tasks. First, how are individual trainees able to achieve personal security and a feeling of belonging among host country nationals without having to apologize for themselves? Second, how can trainees minimize the ambivalence they can expect to feel about the unfamiliar cues to responsibility, authority, and autonomy in their own training program and later intercultural experiences? Third, how can trainees make their experiences a useful educational dimension for their own growth without alienating themselves or others and without withdrawing from the situation? Fourth, how can trainees keep from losing their own identity as members of their home country culture while

they are establishing appropriate cognitive and emotional relationships in the host country? Finally, how can trainees apply
what they have learned after they return home?

One of Hall's (1966) major themes is how our cultural
habits are most effectively hidden from ourselves, even though
they may be quite obvious to others. Along the same lines
there is evidence (Foster, 1965) that those who are *least* effective in their cross-cultural relationships are the same ones who
claim no difficulties in cross-cultural adjustment and who tend
to minimize the importance of cross-cultural dimensions. The
primary task of orientation training is to create an awareness
in a trainee of the specific ways that relationships depend on
assumptions which *may* be very different from one person to
the next.

Culture Shock

Culture shock is a term used to describe the impact of a
new and different culture radically different from a person's
own culture. The symptoms of culture shock include excessive
preoccupation with the cleanliness of one's drinking water,
food and surroundings; great concern over minor pains; excessive anger over delays and other minor frustrations; a fixed
idea that people are taking advantage of or cheating one;
reluctance to learn the language of the host country; a feeling
of hopelessness; and a strong desire to associate with person's
of one's own nationality. Culture shock describes the anxiety
that happens when a person loses all the familiar cues to reality
on which each of us depend. Heiss and Nash (1967) describe
a small degree of anxiety as a normal reaction by strangers in
a new group or culture, but victims of culture shock also experience a decline in inventiveness, spontaneity, and flexibility to
the extent that it interferes with their normal behavior.

Hall (1959) defined culture shock as a "removal or distor-
tion of many of the familiar cues one encounters at home and
the substitution for them of other cues which are strange." The
term was first described in detail by Oberg (1958) who described culture shock as anxiety resulting from losing one's

sense of "when to do what and how." Oberg describes several stages in the process of culture shock. In the first, incubation stage the sojourner may feel genuinely euphoric about the exciting new culture around him. This is followed by a second stage of dealing with crises resulting from the "normal" daily activities that suddenly seem to present insurmountable difficulties, generating hostility toward hosts for being "unreasonable." In the third stage the sojourner begins to understand the host culture and regains a sense of humor. The fourth stage is where the sojourner begins to accept the host culture in a balanced picture of positive and negative aspects. The fifth and final stage occurs when the sojourner returns home and experiences reverse culture shock in the readjustment to the old environment.

The conflict between sojourners' expectations and their own experiences has been described by others in four stages of adjustment. The first stage of fascination is followed by a second stage of hostility against the host culture, followed by a third stage of adjustment and a fourth stage of genuine biculturalism in which the sojourners are able to act in accord with host culture norms. Having experienced culture shock in one culture does not prevent culture shock in the future, although it may provide sojourners with some insights into why they feel as they do (Foster, 1965). Through culture shock sojourners learn ways they are influenced by their own culture and specific ways other persons from other cultures are likewise influenced in their behavior.

Adler (1972) describes seven ways that culture shock contributes to learning.

(1) Learning involves change and movement from one cultural frame of reference to another. Individuals are presented with changes in the cultural landscape.

(2) Culture shock assumes unique importance and meaning to the individuals. Individuals undergo a highly personal experience of special significance to themselves.

(3) Change becomes provocative. Individuals are forced into some form of introspection and self-examination.

(4) Adjustment is extreme in its ups and downs. Individuals undergo various forms of frustration, anxiety, and personal pain.

(5) Confrontation forces personal investigation of relationships. Individuals must deal with the relationships and processes inherent in their situation as outsiders.

(6) New ideas force behavioral experimentation. Individuals must, of necessity, try out new attitudes and behaviors. This becomes a trial-and-error process until appropriate behavioral responses emerge.

(7) The results from step (6) present unlimited opportunity for contrast and comparison. Individuals have at their disposal an unending source of diversity with which they can compare and contrast their own previous experiences.

The greatest impact of culture shock is in learning about and confronting one's own culture. Every culture has its own system of coherence and logic, and all persons are, to some extent, products of their own cultural experience. By comparing the familiar and unfamiliar, sojourners learn something about their own identity. Sojourners learn how their own behavior is grounded in cultural assumptions, values, and beliefs. They further learn how their feelings based on those values affect their relationships with others. These very frustrations and anxiety can lead to self-understanding and personal development. Later chapters on bilingual education will show language to be a primary factor in the process of culture shock, because most of our familiar cues are communicated to us through either language or the nonverbal behaviors closely associated with and interpreted to us through language.

The somewhat similar phenomenon called *role shock* occurs more gradually and is usually longer lasting in its effects. It increases to a peak later in the adjustment process and tends to diminish more slowly, if at all, during the trainee's foreign experience. It is indicated by a building up of ambiguity in the trainee's professional role, reinforced by a sequence of unsuccessful relationships with host nationals, and it inhibits the adjustment of a trainee within the host country hierarchy.

Another notion, labeled by Guthrie (1966, 1975) as *culture fatigue,* was described in relation to Peace Corps volunteers. Its effects tend to be more subtle, characterized by a partial or functional adjustment to the host culture which is never quite completed because Peace Corps volunteers know that they will eventually leave their new culture. The apparent similarities between a trainee's home culture and the host culture are magnified to produce unrealistic expectations and to result in considerable frustration. Szanton (1966) considered culture fatigue to be a sort of exhaustion resulting from the endless number of small adjustments necessary to live in a foreign culture.

Another similar condition is described as the *re-entry crisis,* again described in the literature about Peace Corps returnees and foreign students returning to their home country (Brislin and Van Buren, 1974). The readjustment back home is likely to be even more difficult than going abroad in the first place, all the more so since this adjustment is frequently unexpected. Not only has the trainee changed, but the back-home culture has likewise changed, making it doubly difficult to readjust. People's expectations for returning may have been distorted in an unrealistically favorable direction by their very absence. When they find themselves unable to pick up where they left off or even to start from scratch at some new endeavor, they are likely to experience a re-entry crisis. A program to lessen this re-entry crisis is described in another chapter.

Effective functioning abroad requires that trainees be aware of themselves as a culturally conditioned individual, alert to the differences between themselves and others, aware of the social and emotional needs of themselves and others, and willing to work actively toward meaningful relationships with others whether they are fellow countrymen or host nationals. Rhinesmith (1970) describes this adjustment in the categories of flight, fight, and adaptation. When trainees respond to a new situation through flight they reject the people whom they believe are the cause of their discomfort and withdraw from any opportunity to interact with them. They blame either the locals for being inhospitable or themselves for lacking understanding. They tend to react defensively by moving toward a mode of living that seems more familiar. In some cases this means moving toward the community of their fellow countrymen. In other cases this means flight from their fellow countrymen toward the host culture. In either case the flight alternative results in the trainees' becoming more dependent. When trainees respond to a new culture with hostility and aggression, their reaction is characterized as a fight response, characterized by struggle with the environment to change it in their favor rather than an attempt to understand it. They are likely to react against both fellow countrymen and their hosts with an attitude of counter-dependence that is similarly confining to spontaneous initiatives. The process of cultural adaptation and adjustment requires neither rejecting oneself or others but adapting to the new environment through openness, learning, and behavioral growth toward an interdependent relationship.

The problems of adjustment are continuous throughout the persons' sojourn and even after the individual has returned home. The process of "unfreezing-moving-refreezing" in Lewin field theory jargon describes this life rhythm as a cycle that begins again as the individual and his environment change. In each cycle the unfreezing phase is the most difficult, implying a process of unlearning previously familiar responses. The goal of adjustment implies attitudinal flexibility enabling the individual to exploit the full educational potential of new surroundings. To this degree intercultural sensitivity is not different in nature from interpersonal adjustment. Both require the same skills and the same process through interaction with others, accepting and being able to give accurate feedback about that interaction and contributing toward an atmosphere conducive to intellectual and emotional understanding of each new experience.

The Peace Corps sponsored considerable research on the concept of culture shock which was not continued after the federal funding for Peace Corps training diminished. More research is needed on the effect of culture shock, culture fatigue, and related phenomena experienced by most if not all sojourners at some time. It is also important to seperate this descriptive term from any pejorative evaluation of sojourners who may otherwise look on culture shock as a disease or a weakness in their own personality rather than a rather normal human response to any unique situation. There is evidence that diminished efficiency and increased anxiety resulting from culture shock are expensive in terms of appropriate orientation, and training might minimize that inconvenience.

The Immersion Method

Even when there is no formal training program, such as those discussed in later chapters, the very experience of a cross-cultural sojourn becomes in itself an educational experience. The most frequent mode of cross-cultural training is through everyday experience with persons from other cultures. Cross-cultural contact shapes our responses, sometimes more effectively or profoundly than we realize, as we learn to respond appropriately to persons from other cultures. Goodman (1972) speaks out against separating "learning" from real-life functions and assigning it to schools where a host of artificial problems are introduced that may in fact inhibit learning. Given a real-life situation, Goodman asserts that students will learn all the prerequisite skills that are necessary to be a functioning member of society. The experiences of a tourist or sojourner have a measured effect on his understanding of other cultures. The literature about sojourners in other cultures has described the stages of transition that, in effect, outline a program of training by immersion in another culture. As examples, let us consider two models of foreign students in the United States.

The first model is the course of relationships in which a foreign student must learn different sets of cues and meet different sets of expectations. Eide (1970) describes the process in terms of four communication linkages between foreign students, their home culture, and their host culture.

The first line of communication, relating students to their own home culture, deals with the students' "place" in that culture as occupying a significant role. An important aspect of this relationship is each student's own sense of identity as a product of that culture. Whether a student feels integrated or alienated is at least partly determined by each student's relationship to his own culture before arriving. The second line of communication relates students to their host culture. Students are expected both to adapt to the host culture and to function as a "culture-carrier" from their host culture in ways that frequently conflict with one another. The hosts may focus on strange and unusual aspects of the students' home country, reinforcing stereotypes and resisting any contributory insights foreign students may have about the host culture. The host culture's misinformation about students' home culture will influence the students' ability to exchange knowledge and eventually return home with an accurate perception of their former hosts. The third communication line extends from the host culture to the students. Foreign students from different countries staying in the United States have been treated differentially, with European students being treated more favorably than non-European or Asian students (Eide, 1970). The fourth communication line is between students and their home culture. Students have a special kind of involvement and vested interest relating to prestige by association with the host culture. Students may either support the host culture view when they return home or demonstrate their indigenous identity by playing the host culture down. Fundamental cultural values are less frequently communicated to the home culture—particularly when they involve intimate and personal relationships—than specific technical skills.

Eide described a widely accepted series of assumptions about the intrinsic social value of transferring knowledge across cultural boundaries. First, more knowledge will stretch people's imaginations with a net result of increased tolerance of other cultures, contributing toward stabilization. Second, the diffusion of knowledge about other cultures will lead to a more homogeneous world, mixing the different cultures with one another. Third, the demonstration of how people from different cultures are interdependent on one another might contribute to peace. Fourth, learning about others clarifies knowledge of oneself, contributing to the mutual understanding necessary for a plural society. Fifth, the meeting of cultures and of minds is hoped to enhance the development of all participants in some sort of progress. To say that intercultural communications have intrinsic social value, however, is quite different from demonstrating that it fulfills that function in face-to-face interaction. (Triandis et al., 1972).

Conway (1969) describes a second model that provides a global view of foreign student changing levels of self-satisfaction in a *U* curve which extends into a *W* curve hypothesis

(Lysgaard, 1955; Sewel and Davidson, 1961). This hypothesis has been widely used to describe cross-cultural adjustment.

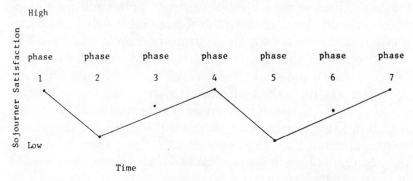

Figure 1
The W Curve Hypothesis

The hypotheses are as follows: when foreign students arrive in this country there is a novelty effect and the promise of significant benefit from their education experience that can provide a high level of satisfaction. They are satisfied to function in the role of an observer and are often perceived as something of an interesting novelty by the generally receptive academic community. These and other factors contribute to a halo or honeymoon effect during the earliest part of the experience.

As the novelty wears off, areas of conflict appear that place demands for accommodation on foreign students, and the students experience the culture shock of their stranger/foreigner role. It is during this second phase that the serious problems arise.

The process of adjustment begins to alleviate culture shock in the third phase with his more successful adjustment, resulting in rewards of increased satisfaction as students begin to realize some of the earlier goals of their expectations. Their fluency in English and familiarity with social roles has increased to facilitate coping with their stranger/foreigner role.

By about the time students are ready to return home their level of satisfaction may have been restored. Restored levels of satisfaction depend, of course, on their being successful in attaining their academic goals. The prospect of being reunited with family and friends and the novelty effect of returning home likewise contribute to their high level of satisfaction. These first four phases are described as the *U* curve of adjustment.

In phase five students are faced with difficulties of readjustment and acceptance in their new roles. This phase is all the more difficult for students who do not expect problems of adjustment to their home culture, and who fail to recognize the ways in which they have been changed by their foreign experience. Numerous practical problems of readjustment arise just as they did when they arrived in the United States (Brislin and Van Buren 1974).

If students are able to adjust satisfactorily, the sixth phase will provide opportunity for establishing themselves in a satisfactory role, providing that such a role is available, making use of their newly learned skills and enjoying some increased prestige.

The seventh phase provides for re-establishing permanent rewards of acceptance resulting in a high level of satisfaction. Those who are unable to attain this level of satisfaction frequently emigrate permanently to the United States or some other culture, resulting in a phenomena of a brain drain from the less developed to the more developed countries.

Torrey et al. (1970) cite an unpublished study by Selby and Woods (1962) that relates measures of academic and social adjustment more to the schedule of academic examinations and vacations than to the adjustment process. Torrey concludes that the *U* curve hypothesis was originally based on adjustment by immigrants over a long period of time and may not apply to student's short-term adjustment. The student's unique situation demands that they adjust to an academic culture of the university community as well as the outside society.

Cultural Futurology

There is some question about whether cross-cultural orientation programs will be more or less popular in the future than they are now. There is some question about whether this field has a future, although increased cross-cultural contact suggests that it does indeed.

Useem and Useem (1955, 1963, 1968), in their earlier publications, have referred to the mutually compatible position between two cultures as a third culture, and that this is a component of modern man's condition. To have cross-cultural communication, the participants of a modern plural society must meet on a cultural common ground. This binational alternative is defined as the complex of patterns learned and shared by cultures with both a Western and an Eastern orientation who are regularly interacting. This process, accelerated by technological development, has direct implications for intercultural training to survive in a plural society.

At a 1970 conference of the American Anthropological Association on "Cultural Futurology", Maruyama (1970) compared cultural change to technological change and described the differences. Cultural futurology aims at developing scientific, experimental, and engineering attitudes rather than the simple teaching of scientific data. The cultural goals are generated by people rather than imposed on them; these goals are heterogenous and diverse, they are changing and not constant, and they deal with people instead of objects. The guiding of cultural change faces distinct handicaps in that future cultures are not yet observable. They can not be easily predicted by extrapolating from the past, nor do those changes occur spontaneously, but rather require guidance by people.

Maruyama (1966) describes persons who are brought up with a dependency on one authority, one theory, and one truth as victims of monopolarization. Monopolarized persons tend to be trapped in one way of thinking, believing that theirs is the universal way. They are trapped in an inflexible structure that resists adaptation to alternative ways of thinking. This is contrasted with what Maruyama (1970) calls *trans-spection,* which is an effort to put oneself in the mind of another person. One tries to believe what the other person believes and assume what the other person assumes. Going beyond analytical understanding and even empathy, trans-spection is a process of learning a foreign belief, assumption, or perspective and the feelings of a foreign context and consequences in such a way that the practitioner temporarily believes what the other person believes. Through cross-cultural exposure, people can be liberated to cope with constant change and generate non-hierarchical cultural patterns of exchange. The orientation techniques covered by Triandis (1975), reviewed later in this book, have the "see as other people see" concept as a central goal.

Collequium III held at Bellagio, Italy in 1972 took as its theme Cultural Relations for the Future (Braisted, 1972). The conference focused on four factors and their implications for cultural relations.

(1) The interdependency of peoples is an inherent part of all basic problems and an important aspect of the developing life of nations.

(2) New developments in science, religion, arts, and philosophy which are creating changing views of man, his society, and his world require critical examination.

(3) Accelerating technological change produces cultural problems and creates new opportunities for imaginative cooperative activities.

(4) Urban, population, ecological, and other problems call for new ideas and action.

In the concluding portion of the report of the conference study groups suggested ten areas of necessary change to "reconstitute the human community."

(1) The human community is not one culture for the whole world but many cultures requiring transcendence of a psychology of dominance by the power of science and technology.

(2) The curse of cultural relations has been the incubus of a dualistic view of the world divided between the powerful and the weak, the donor and the recipient, the dominant and the dependent.

(3) The future does not lie in remaking culture in a single mold, but in discovering and reinforcing local strengths, revitalizing traditions, as well as giving birth to new cultures and patterns.

(4) New patterns of relationships and institutions, of social and political inventions are needed for all aspects of cultural relations.

(5) We are in a state of cultural crises, conscious of rapid

change and aware that we share a common plight to depend on one another.

(6) We have come to realize and recognize new purposes and new approaches to problem solving in the issues of population, disease, the environment, and conflict resolution.

(7) Central to the long-range tasks of reconstituting the human community is a more imaginative awareness of the moral and spiritual potentialities of man, drawing on old and new concepts, bad and good, to influence the changing world order.

(8) Reconstituting the human community involves new roles, undreamed of previously, requiring us to restructure roles and opportunities.

(9) Understanding the human community means facing and welcoming inescapable differences in the world community as resources for change.

(10) Despite cultural differences there are still aspects from which we can derive strength and which require our respect in the mode of *e pluribus unum.*

We are coming to know more about the process by which beliefs, values, and attitudes concerning the world outside the United States are formed and changed, providing the basis for a developmental approach to personal growth and allowing educational decisions to be based on more adequate evidence. The notion of the international content of education is being broadened from a technical speciality to a globalized curriculum applied to all learning which reflexively relates to persons from all cultures. Finally, there is increased recognition for a total framework, including more precise objectives, systems of continuous assessment, and evaluation and formulation of educational strategies providing the criteria for and means of international education.

Technology's contribution to cross-cultural training is evident in the PEACESAT (Pan Pacific Education and Communication Experiments by Satellite) project initiated in 1969 at the University of Hawaii. This pilot satellite communications system has been operating since 1971 using the National Aeronautics and Space Administration's Applications Technology Satellite, ATS-1. The system of locally financed and operated terminals include New Zealand, Fiji, Papua New Guinea, Kingdom of Tonga, American Samoa, Saipan in the Trust Territory of the Pacific Islands, and the South Pacific Commission in New Caledonia, with six additional sites under construction (Bystrom, 1974). The objectives of the PEACE-SAT project are (1) to determine what communications can be developed to improve health, education, and community services in the Pacific with the availability of low-cost satellite and other communications links and (2) to conduct a series of pilot communication activities both international and U.S. Pacific, in which satellite communication is applied to health care, education, and community programs.

The PEACESAT facilities have been used in a variety of ways to provide cross-cultural training. Decision-making conferences involving administrators at several locations have allowed joint discussions on a regular basis. Professional and in-service training programs have been organized to include the sparsely populated areas of the Pacific as well as metropolitan Honolulu. Classroom instruction through university courses for credit have been scheduled with students from the Pacific basin participating via radio communication. Community development seminars have been organized and have shown promise for future programming. Consultation and report arrangements have been useful both in diagnostic consulting and for the instant availability of emergency or urgent communications between locations on short notice. Finally, high-priority social service agencies have used the network for a variety of special purposes, with plans to develop programs through the University of the South Pacific Network Intercultural Division and the Speech Communication Association International.

Several national organizations have also recognized the importance of cross-cultural training. A special committee of the International Communication Association Intercultural Commission has prepared a report outlining needs for the future. The section of their report dealing with worldwide training identifies eleven priorities for cross-cultural training. Their recommendations include:

1. Development of international and intercultural cooper-

ation for training through existing organizations.

2. Linking language and cultural training.

3. Training for business and industrial personnel as well as professionals in religious, academic, and other areas.

4. Development of substructures on intercultural communications within existing organizations.

5. Developing international publications.

6. Cataloguing existing resources on a worldwide basis.

7. Development of a viable information retrieval system.

8. Developing methods for evaluating and certifying each trainer.

9. Developing instruments for measuring training effects.

10. Practical application of culture-related data through research and training.

11. Increasing worldwide awareness of intercultural communications needs, resources, and objectives. (Bystrom et al., 1974).

A second specific example of organizational awareness is the inaugural conference of the Society for Intercultural Education Training and Research (SIETAR) in February 1975 (Hoopes, 1975). SIETAR is a professional association designed to promote the development of the field of intercultural communication and foster its application to the practical problems of those involved in intercultural areas. The conference allowed 230 of the leaders in this field to exchange ideas in the theory and practice of cross-cultural training.

In describing the future of intercultural education Harms (1974) distinguishes between TELECOMNET, or the revolutionary advances in communications technology, and TRANSCOMNET, relating to the increased opportunity for persons to move from one country to another around the world. These systems share two important characteristics: first, they are centered in the northern hemisphere; second, a small number of large cities serve as regional communication centers. Where people live in the world determines access to both communication networks, so that the opportunities for cross-cultural exchange are unevenly distributed. These limitations have been more apparent as world communication technology advances, as the numbers of world organizations increases, and as intranational local cultures are revived in an emerging emphasis on biculturalism.

We are involved in a worldwide communication revolution in which monocultural understandings of human communication are dangerously inadequate. In exploring the opportunities to communicate we need to explore the effect of population growth and urban concentrations and patterns of migration: What are the implications of major powers controlling communication networks for the goal of world peace? What technological developments are still necessary for communication across cultures and how do we train one another to utilize those communications?

The first step is to specify our communication needs and then to establish those needs as rights. In a total sense any person's being denied the right to communicate violates the rights of all the rest of us. Control of the communication media, computerized thought control, and the capability for electronic surveillance are as great a threat to us as the more easily understood dangers of nuclear annihilation. Cross-cultural orientation is an important aspect of the future task for cross-cultural training. Numerous national organizations have already become aware of the need for such training in culture-related variables as a transition step between cultural isolation from the past and some point in the future when the cross-cultural component will be a part of every educational curricula.

Conclusion

We have reviewed concepts essential to understanding the training designs and identifying the target audiences to be discussed in the next two sections of this book. We are assuming that there are many good reasons for training, providing that training meets certain criteria of excellence. It is important, for example, that the assumptions we are making about other cultures be tested against empirical data. Does self-awareness, for example, contribute to cultural sensitivity? At present the data are very inadequate. Training goals need to be reasonable, realistic, and measurable to determine whether they have indeed been accomplished. Training programs must contribute toward changes in the real world outside the training classroom itself. Support systems need to be nurtured to reward trainees and encourage programs that do indeed facilitate cultural adjustment. In order to build on previous programs it is essential both that the training programs be rigorously evaluated and that some sort of follow-up on what happens to trainees be emphasized. In the absence of clear supporting data, it is important that both general and specific approaches of intercultural training be available to target populations.

Although there is research suggesting that failure overseas can be traced to intercultural adjustment problems, there is no clear solution to remedy that situation. In a general sense we know, for example, that situations in which the same stimulus requires a different response (such as the Skaggs-Robinson hypothesis) are the most difficult, and we can concentrate on those stimuli with special attention. We know that persons are most likely to evaluate others from the point of view of their own self-reference criterion and that training can prepare them for the results of that kind of behavior. We know that the barriers of language, gestures, preconceptions, prejudgment, and anxiety are likely to inhibit intercultural communication, and we can prepare trainees for these kinds of problems. The field of intercultural training can, therefore, make a contribution with some assurance of benefit.

What happens if sojourners are not trained but simply immersed into another culture to "sink or swim" on their own? This more traditional approach is still perhaps the most popular and widely used, although it is obviously not the most efficient or effective. "Doing what comes naturally" varies from one culture to another and can be a perilous guideline. We might look at foreign students coming to this country from their home country for examples of the adjustment process without benefit of training. There are stages of adjustment and development that provide useful benchmarks of progress through the haphazard contingencies of the immersion method. The process of training can be called orientation, just as the process of cultural shock can be described as disorientation, removing an individual from his familiar cues and surroundings. The term has been borrowed to describe less dramatic and perhaps more commonly experienced stress known as culture fatigue, role shock, or future shock, each term describing the accommodation of an individual to a new and unfamiliar value system. Experience is a good teacher, but it is not the only alternative available.

It is important to realize that cross-cultural training has not been widely applied to the large numbers of technical assistants going abroad, not to mention persons in our own country immersed in another culture. The expense of training has been considered a luxury, even when compared with the expense of individual failure, which itself was frequently considered an unnecessary expenditure of time and money. There is a need for all of us to sharpen our intercultural skills in order to accommodate the cultures of the future, which are likely to be totally different than any cultural system we are now experiencing. Those who have developed skills for adaptation will survive the rapid transition and change we are now experiencing.

As readers consider the training models and designs of the next section, we would like them to keep some of the assumptions we are making in mind to help evaluate those aspects most useful in various training situations. Readers might identify parts of the designs that will be most beneficial to their needs and situation, even though they may not find any of the designs applicable as a total unit. Readers may then derive their own uniquely suitable approach for training in an eclectic adaptation. Another helpful way to use this book would be to consider the target audiences in the third section of this book and to look for themselves among the populations discussed. Readers might finally try to identify the ways in which they might personally benefit from inter-cultural training.

2

ORIENTATION MODELS

A Cross-Cultural Interaction Design

To begin our coverage of programs, models, and designs that have been used for cross-cultural orientations, we review a multifaceted system that combines selection and training. The best aspects and lessons of all the trainees from various programs to be reviewed are summarized at the end of this chapter. Chaffee (1971) has devised a systems design for the selection and training of persons across cross-cultural lines, with special attention to people with technical skills. He applies the basic research in communications to organize training and selection criteria. Chaffee is critical of selection criteria that accept whomever is available, or criteria that lead to selection of people whom authorities would like to see removed from the parent organization for a year or two, or people whose turn has conveniently come up for reassignment. By contrast, more attention should be given to the individual's qualifications, the family's adjustment abroad, and other intercultural factors. The consequences of improper selection are

expensive in the long run, with hidden costs such as realloca-
tion of personnel, midterm reassignment, or failure on the job.

The typical process of training which Chaffee criticizes
is most often through the use of reading materials and is
not accompanied by systematic intercultural interaction or
job-oriented instruction. Both the needs of the individual
and those of the organization can be met in an adequate
training design. In the approach Chaffee recommends, information and factual data complement instruction on cultural differences between the United States and the target
culture. Trainees are encouraged to become more aware of
themselves through a variety of cross-cultural training techniques. A variety of training modes are available that could
be tailored to the needs of the sponsor, the trainee, and his
or her family. Unfortunately, as Chaffee points out, training
performance is almost never considered as part of the selection criteria and is only begun after the act of selection,
without really contributing to the selection decision itself.
The current (1974–1975) Peace Corps rationale for this process is that selection (and all this implies) too easily interferes with the training function that focuses on the preparation of an individual to deal with another culture (Harris,
1975). But where training may have improved because of
the reduction or elimination of the stresses of selection,
there seems to have been a loss in quality control. How can
both aspects be effectively continued?

The selection and training system described in the following 12 steps suggest one approach for designing a selection and
training program where these two functions are integral to
one another (descriptions of steps 1 to 12 adapted from
Chaffee, 1971).

Step 1
*Study the Technical Requirements to Determine a Person's
Qualifications.* In determining these requirements, the fol-
lowing should be considered:

(a) Individuals selected for overseas work must be extremely
competent in the required technical area because they will

be operating in a foreign environment without the benefit of backup by trusted colleagues.

(b) They must be able to adapt technology to possibly primitive conditions, i.e., using bailing wire instead of machine bolts.

Step 2
Personnel Unacceptable for this Overseas Assignment. If at any time during the selection process we are forced back to this point we should either find new personnel who are acceptable or give up the work. And it should be emphasized that it is far better (and in the end far cheaper) to give up the work at this point than to accept a project with the idea of "bluffing one's way through."

Step 3
Are the Families of the Technically Qualified Willing to Go Abroad? Or Are the Technically Qualified Willing to Go Without Family? And if So Will This Cause Problems at Home? The important factor to be considered here is that the family often makes or breaks a technical man abroad. Overseas the family is exposed in a way it seldom is at home, and the chances of family strain are greatly increased. All of these can affect technical performance on the job. Every care must be taken to ensure that at a minimum the family will pose as little problem as possible and prefereably will be an asset to the technical man during his foreign assignment. If the family situation poses a problem, then the person under consideration should be considered unacceptable for the position.

Step 4
Determine the Physical Requirements Necessary for the Work and the World Area. Many a good technical person and many a willing family have gone abroad only to be ineffective and unable to accomplish their missions because of physical ills. This is a real and serious problem which should at least be considered during the selection process.

Step 5
If Possible Determine the Reason the Person Wants to Go Abroad. Probably no one should be rejected for overseas work solely on the basis of why they want to go—with the

exception of those who want to go for a lark. (An overseas assignment may be interesting and even fun—but it will very likely never be a lark.) For example those who go for money or class status may do as good—or even a better job than those who go out of sense of mission. This is just one more subjective factor that should be considered in context with other selection criteria (Cleveland et al. 1960).

Step 6
Determine the Traits Best Suited for the Work and Area. Both technical personnel and their families should be considered in terms of such traits. With respect to personal traits, it should be emphasized that if an individual has a small problem in the United States, it may very well be magnified overseas. If, for example an individual shows a tendency toward instability with his co-workers in America, it is likely that this tendency will be magnified overseas. Another factor to be considered when screening personnel is that the desirable traits should be almost "second nature" to the candidate. It is doubtful that an intensive training program would result in lasting basic changes in the area of personality, attitudes and beliefs. It seems that the candidate must already "have it" or the situation is hopeless because of time/schedule pressures. All these factors contribute to still another subjective weight which should be added to the overall selection process.

Step 7
Are the Remaining Candidates Available for Assignment or Are They Already Committed? And If Committed, Can they be Made Available? If we can state that the personnel are available then we have no immediate problem. If we cannot, then we must ask how they can be made available. The most important reason for not beginning the selection process with the question of availability, as is frequently done, is that such a question asked early often automatically eliminates the best qualified.

Step 8
Train Both the Technical Personnel and Their Families. The important factor to note at this point is that training should be for both the technical personnel and their families. Of

course, various training possibilities can be found throughout this book.

Step 9

Evaluate Training Performance. We tend to place esteem on the evaluation of training for sports and other activities, but we frequently seem to ignore altogether, or at least play down, evaluation of training for overseas assignments. Most frequently by the time training is given, selection has already taken place. The evaluation of training therefore is not usually a part of the selection process. We believe this is wrong. That is why we recommend an integrated selection and training system.

Step 10

Select Personnel and Assign them to a Foreign Post. The staff for the overseas assignment should not be selected until this step has been reached. All the remaining candidates at this point should be qualified for the position.

Step 11

Plan for Post Training and Evaluation of Technical Personnel and their Families. Every attempt should be made to give the technical personnel and their families in-country orientation and training.

Step 12

Return Unsatisfactory Personnel to States. It is far better to admit to a personnel-selection mistake, if one has been made, and to send the unsatisfactory people home rather than to try to "bluff" through with someone who may upset the entire project.

Chaffee's system provides a framework. Without any framework at all, as is quite often the case, the training tends to drift from method to method, allowing the techniques to become the end themselves with little understanding of what is being attempted. The techniques should be suited to the target culture and the trainees themselves. Such a program will require considerable amounts of time and money in the initial stages of international placement, but it may save still more money in avoiding mistakes later, as well as contributing to the general well-being of a trainee.

The Intellectual Model

Although there is much criticism of the "intellectual" or university classroom model for intercultural education (Harrison and Hopkins, 1967) the bulk of cross-cultural orientation continues to occur in university classrooms around the country. A list of classroom syllabi on courses was compiled recently by Prosser (1974) who includes more than fifty courses concerned directly with cross-cultural communications. Although this listing represents only a small portion of courses being taught, it demonstrates the impressive effort by universities to respond in the area of intercultural education. This may be partially explained by the demand among university students for courses in this area. Most of the trainers or facilitators of cross-cultural groups are also attached to a university, even though some of their training groups may be outside the university. In the emphasis on "experiential" approaches to cross-cultural training, it is important to recognize a need for more rigorous content-related approaches to develop the field or area of cross-cultural orientation.

The two orientations do not exclude one another. Programs outside the university may also have required readings, tests, or evaluation procedures, and a particular topic may be taught, just as university courses may include experiential exercises or unstructured opportunities. To that extent the division by Harrison and Hopkins (1967; reviewed elsewhere in this book) may have done the field a disservice by contrasting the intellectual and experiential approaches in a somewhat artificial division, in fact a good program will incorporate aspects of both approaches. There is ample evidence that simulations increase motivation and involvement, but they have been less effective than straight lectures for conveying content knowledge about a topic.

The weakness of an intellectual model has been its tendency to generalize artificially and abstractly about a topic, a culture, or a process with insufficient attention to the real situation. Talking about "poverty" and being "poor" are very much different from one another. There has been an elitist bias associated with the intellectual model; this approach can be a substitute for direct experience with persons from the culture being "studied." Members of the target culture have also, understandably, objected to being "studied" as curious examples of an esoteric viewpoint. The classic example ridiculing this intellectual approach is an *American Anthropologist* article about a "Nacirema" (American spelled backwards) culture which is hardly recognizable to the native American reader.

Several programs have incorporated aspects of the intellectual model outside the classroom setting. One such example is the InterCulture Associates (Box 277, Thompson, Connecticut 06277), a private organization developing curriculum and materials on intercultural education, who have organized a series of workshops. The objective of these workshops is for each participant to work out a personal statement of their own goals for intercultural education. The technique used is to give that person firsthand experience with the target culture through curriculum materials on that culture. InterCulture Associates is a group of professional educators developing, publishing, and distributing curriculum materials for culture learning. They have published, imported, and distributed books both from and about the cultures being studied, developed filmstrips and slides, and are developing multimedia artifact units on various cultures. These materials are used in their own workshops and are available for persons wanting to incorporate them into other programs.

The A. K. Rice Institute, the Washington School of Psychiatry, and the Department of Psychiatry, Yale University are organizing workshops like those developed at the Tavistock Institute of Human Relations in London, England. The focus of these workshops is on the effects of authority on the participant and others, with special attention to understanding covert processes in groups. Within the groups, participants examine their own values, their effect on others, and their effect on him in a group situation; reactions to authority and power relationships; group boundaries; roles in a group; and self-disclosure. The participant learns about the structures and processes of social institutions through the way in which authority is distributed in a group. The group itself, therefore, becomes a subject for study rather than any individual within the group, which sharply differentiates this design from sensitivity training or encounter groups. The focus is on problems encountered in the exercise of authority.

Howell (1974) outlines the requirements for teaching intercultural communication in a classroom.

1. Communication theory must be utilized.

2. The course must incorporate and not ignore ethnic and cultural resources among participating students.

3. In-class and out-of-class resources should be included.

4. Multicultural *methods* as well as multicultural content should be exemplified.

5. Experiential learning should supplement the learning of information.

6. Boundaries of academic disciplines are crossed as necessary to define the problems discussed.

7. Local problems are not neglected but included in a global perspective.

These guidelines accurately incorporate a balance of approaches to enrich a classroom experience using the intellectual model.

Minnesota EDU-521 Human Relations Training

Cross-cultural orientation programs have been developed to meet a need in public schools. In connection with the desegregation and integration of public schools some states have begun to require in-service training in intercultural communications. The State Board of Education in Minnesota has passed regulation EDU-521, which requires all applicants for certificates in education that are issued or renewed on or after July 1, 1973, to have completed a training program in areas of human relations. Essentially, the regulation stipulates four competency areas an applicant should develop: (1) to understand the contributions and life styles of the various racial, cultural, and economic groups in our society; (2) to recognize and deal with dehumanizing biases, discrimination, and prejudices; (3) to create learning environments that contribute to the self-esteem of all persons and to positive interpersonal relations; (4) to respect human diversity and personal rights. Similar requirements are being considered by many of the other state legislatures across the country as the importance of intercultural relations is becoming apparent.

Filla and Clark (1973) have described competencies demonstrating an awareness of the concerns and needs important to the purposes of the human relations requirement. Although these sample competencies do not claim to be the "best" statements or to be "all inclusive," they do provide some examples of applying the theory of human relations to the practical problems of human relations. The first cluster of competencies aims at understanding the contributions and life styles of various clultural groups. The effective program shoud be able to: (1)demonstrate knowledge of the process of socio-cultural development and change; (2) demonstrate knowledge of the characteristics and history of cultural groups within American society; (3) demonstrate knowledge of life styles that differ from those of the majority culture and identify ways in which these life styles serve the participants in the culture, (4) demonstrate knowledge of the activities and contributions of outstanding leaders, spokesmen and organizations from these groups; (5) understand and recognize the various subcultures of society; (6) develop a knowledge base for assessing the racial climate in America; (7) demonstrate and develop an attitude of social responsibility and cooperation concerning intergroup relations and harmony: (8) write a unit of study on a culture that is different from their own; (9) incorporate information about people who are culturally and economically different in the institutional program; (10) live with persons from a minority culture; (11) observe and teach in a school with persons from a minority culture.

These sample competencies demonstrate a balance of congnitive, or "knowing" goals, affective or "feeling" goals and behavioral or "doing" goals. The process of understanding applied to an intercultural training design needs to include all three aspects among their competency objectives. Likewise the competencies demonstrate a balance of "learning" new ideas or skills and "unlearning" the obsolete, inaccurate views or misinformation from previous experience. A balanced program also needs to include persons from different cultural backgrounds, beyond the narrowly defined viewpoint of any single culture. The resources for learning about inter-cultural communication are the persons themselves from those cultures being studied who are readily available in the trainee's "target" population. Another type of resource person is the individual who has successfully lived in another culture.

A second set of competencies involves the recognition of dehumanizing biases, discrimination or prejudices and the skills to change them in the trainee. The participant who completes an effective program should be able to (1) demonstrate knowledge of work, phrases, or labels that are viewed as derogatory by specific cultural groups; (2) demonstrate understanding of the importance of positive self-image for individual pupils and of types of experiences that hinder the development of positive self-image; (3) demonstrate ability to counteract examples of negative discrimination as they occur in school; (4) demonstrate ability to recognize one's own attitudes and feelings and to control and use them in positive ways; (5) understand and accept the pupil's right to withdraw from specific activities; (6) demonstrate the ability to recognize and deal with conflict situations involving values and rights; (7) demonstrate the ability to see and to propose alternatives to bias, discrimination, and prejudice; (8) evaluate, judge, and select teaching materials for use in the classroom and library (this includes recognizing stereotype statements in such materials and developing a course of studies that includes human relations activity and cultural contributions of minorities); (9) identify and describe examples of biased behavior and prepare a strategy for dealing with this behavior in a positive way for presentation to her small group; (10) recognize biases and prejudices in others; (11) recognize biases and prejudices that are injurious to others.

The primary benefits of intercultural communications

training are to increase a trainee's degree of freedom, not to change the trainee in ways he/she may not want to be changed. There is a significant difference between understanding or accepting another's values and choosing to adopt those values for oneself. Bias, discrimination, and prejudice have become "bad" words in our vocabulary, without recognition of the benefits derived from cultural stereotypes that contribute to our sense of cultural identity. The emphasis in these competencies is on being aware of our cultural bias and then making a deliberate rather than accidental decision about whether we wish to retain those prejudices. Cultural bias becomes most dangerous when it is implicit in the attitudes of an individual or policies of an institution without sufficient consideration of consequences.

A third cluster of competencies relates to creating learning environments that contribute to the self-esteem of all persons and to positive inter-personal relations. The graduate of a good training program should be able to: (1) demonstrate ability to assist students to experience success and to learn in a variety of ways; (2) demonstrate ability to communicate effectively with all pupils and to make positive contributions to the learning environment; (3) demonstrate ability to allow honest emotions to be expressed in the classroom and to understand the effect of one's behavior on others; (4) demonstrate the ability to create programs in which children can learn in a variety of ways; (5) demonstrate the ability to de-emphasize competition and comparison in learning and to subordinate marks to learning; (6) demonstrate the ability to understand communication systems and the use of the self for modeling purposes; (7) demonstrate the ability to oppose rules and regulations that are unfair or that infringe on students rights; (8) identify human relations problems and accept ownership of each problem as in a learning situation; (9) identify those areas of understanding in which a student is deficient as well as those in which a student has made progress; (10) develop the ability and the habit of checking one's understanding of cognitive material communicated by another; (11) describe another's behavior without making assumptions and interpretations about attitudes, motives, or character; (12) discriminate between expressing feelings and describing feelings (to be able to send clear "I feel" messages instead of "you are" messages); (13) demonstrate listening skills that will not shift the ownership of the problem from the student to the instructor unless appropriate; (14) design group activities that develop mutual interdependence and independence and self-direction; (15) apply one-to-one interpersonal communication models; (16) accept a pupil's language pattern as worthy and consider it as the starting point for communication and instruction; (17) utilize spontaneous classroom conflict situations as opportunities to demonstrate problem solving techniques.

The progress of a plural society depends on whether power is shared on an equitable basis. The contrary policy has been one of "helping" persons less "fortunate" than ourselves whom we have labeled as "disadvantaged" rather than to share power with them on any equitable basis. Chessler and Don (1970) cite some of the ways in which a traditional learning environment frustrates intercultural communications. The teacher must first deal with preconceived views of people from other cultures that have generated both antagonism and fear as defenses against open communications both between teacher and student and between student and other students. Programs of preservice training have not been sufficient to prepare teachers for coping with cultural aspects of education or to provide a supporting collegial community. The implicit constraints of white-dominated "Anglo" values and the militant response of separatists both politicize intercultural communications and prevent the open exchange of learning.

A fourth cluster of competencies teaches respect for human diversity and personal rights. The graduate should be able to: (1) demonstrate awareness that each people and each group is unique and has an inalienable right to individuality; (2) demonstrate willingness to encounter persons considerably different from oneself; (3) demonstrate respect for diversity in opinions, attitudes, appearances, abilities, and behaviors; (4) demonstrate willingness to support the right of due process for all people; (5) enable the student to make personal and professional decisions characterized by respect and acceptance of others; (6) enable the student to compare and contrast the

value system, life style, and contributions of a specified
minority group with those of the majority group within the
society; (7) demonstrate the ability to listen accurately; (8)
demonstrate the skills and techniques of working with pupils
and show ability in guiding their development; (9) demonstrate the ability to accept human differences as positive values; (10) understand and demonstrate acceptance of different
language styles; (11) design classroom activities that promote
a growth in human diversity and personal rights; (12) identify
the aspects of cultural pluralism that are most difficult for people to accept; (13) affirm one's belief in cultural pluralism pub-
licly.

The training process as described by these competencies
goes through several stages in progression. First, the trainee
assesses personal motivation and relationship to the target intercultural population in some specific ways. Each person
needs to know oneself, know the target population, and know
his or her own limitations in bringing about desired changes.
Second, the trainee needs to design a plan for change, identifying the need for specific changes. Participants need to know
friends from enemies when making changes, learn the attitudes of populations toward those changes, and understand
the methods that are likely to produce changes. Third, the
trainee needs to define a task, considering both the good and
bad aspects. Further, there is a need to develop change-agent
skills, to project the impact of proposed changes, to clarify
one's own role in relationship with the target population, and
to develop a sensitivity to the target population's perception
of his or her role. Fourth, the trainee needs to plan an approach involving members of the target population in the
planning and to develop the necessary techniques or tools. The
trainee should try out parts of the plan, allow for feedback and
continuous re-evaluation of the task, and limit the objectives
to a few specifics that can later be evaluated in terms of specific
outcomes. Fifth, the trainee needs to carry out the plan.
Trainees need to build and maintain morale, monitor the
effects of changes on the target population, and maintain congruence between methods and goals. Sixth, the trainee needs
to evaluate or assess progress in the project. The person needs

to anticipate problems and diagnose the reason for unexpected results, then modify the methods and otherwise learn from mistakes. Finally, the trainee needs to ensure continuity and the transfer of positive results apply what was learned through training. Trainees need to motivate others with responsibility to participate toward a solution, to generate a wider support for changes, and to appreciate the contribution of others in applying the training results to the target population.

Intercultural Communications Workshop

The Intercultural Communications Workshop (ICW) is a form of human relations training involving small groups of foreign and United States nationals. This approach to cross-cultural orientation has developed in universities in which larger numbers of foreign students provide a resource for face-to-face intercultural education with American students. David Hoopes of the Intercultural Communications Network at the University of Pittsburgh is generally credited with coordinating the ICW approach through materials published by the network and circulated to persons working with foreign students. This approach is designed to provide participants with opportunities to move along various stages of a continuum, beginning with simple awareness to a deeper understanding, appreciation, and, finally, acceptance of cultural differences and similarities (Alther, 1970). The basic stages of this continuum are based on a deeper penetration into the cultures and an increasing tendency to identify, discuss, and predict the culturally influenced aspects of the opinions, behavior, values, and attitudes of the individuals in the group.

The beginning stage is characterized by an emerging awareness of other cultures. Awareness may come from the sensing similarities or differences, the gaining of limited information about others, self-examination, or the developing of facile stereotypes as hypotheses for "testing" and discussion. Within a workshop participants achieve this stage in the initial sessions as a result of discussing differing expectations for the workshop, having foreign students give some of their impressions of their initial experiences in the United States, or having American students give their initial impressions of foreign countries. An expression of differences will occur, although the participants may or may not agree with the cultural basis for interpreting these differences. Group members frequently argue that differences are individual rather than cultural. However, it is the task of the leader or resource person to use the material "produced" in the group and to assist the members in examining the underlying cultural differences and similarities. ICWs with only two cultural groups represented have an advantage in differentiating cultural from interpersonal differences more easily than multicultural groups in which cultural differences are usually more complicated to identify.

Cultural penetration is characterized by the development of tolerance and respect for differences among individuals of other cultures and by a readiness to explore different ways of meeting these needs. By this time participants should be able to think critically in regard to international problems and share intercultural misunderstandings. Individuals from cultures in which the focus is on the group rather than the individual or maintaining the harmony of the community are likely to feel extremely uncomfortable discussing personal experiences and feelings. On the other hand, persons coming from cultures in which the individual is the focal point are likely to desire personal confrontations with expression, discussion, and interpretations of feelings. The leader must work to maintain coordination of content and process while simultaneously assisting the members to reach the characteristics marking this stage of intercultural understandings.

Empathy with persons of other cultures leads to a sense of emotional involvement and a realistic interpretation of cultural differences as the basis of comprehending underlying principles. Empathy may also illuminate the interdependence of nations and the necessity for cooperation as the basis for human relationships. Ultimately and ideally, cross-cultural involvement would be characterized by self-appreciation beyond empathetic understanding, incorporating those values of other cultures that have meaning for others.

Workshops seek to effect change on two dimensions. The first of these dimensions relates to changes within each individual participant's perception of self. It is assumed that each participant's behavior is guided by those culture-related factors that inadvertently affect his/her opinions, attitudes, and decisions, as well as those culture-related factors which each one deliberately allows to affect his/her opinions, attitudes, and decisions. The workshop seeks to achieve congruence between the participant's actual behavior and preferred behavior in cross-cultural situations. In this way the participant is able to achieve greater freedom to choose whether to follow a behavior mode as an outgrowth of higher cultural values in forming opinions and attitudes and in making decisions.

The second of these dimensions relate to interaction with other individuals from other cultures, particularly individual participants in the workshop. It is assumed that those individuals' behavior is guided by culture-related factors that they deliberately choose to allow to affect opinions, attitudes, and decisions and which are recognized by the participants as culture related. The workshop seeks to achieve internal congruence between the inadvertent and deliberate effect that culture-related factors may have on each participant's behavior and increased understanding of incongruence for persons of other cultures.

The ICW attempts to achieve these objectives through several methods.

1. Readings are related to the intellectual model of intercultural communication research.

2. Role-playing exercises allow participants to rehearse the role of another person or play their own role in specific interaction. Role playing allows the participants to simulate the experience they will have in another culture and to experience themselves as products of his culture.

3. Critical incidents describe difficult and often conflicting situations that occur between people of different cultural backgrounds when they interact.

4. Communication exercises are designed to facilitate the process of communicating interpersonally with person from different cultures by learning appropriate skills.

The ICW can be viewed as one form of human-relations training in small groups involving foreign and American participants. As Alther (1971) points out, the ICW differs from sensitivity training programs in several ways:

1. An ICW by definition includes participants from more than one culture.

2. The primary objective in ICW is to increase awareness among the participants of the role their cultural backgrounds play in influencing their values, their behavior, and their perceptions of the world around them.

3. Such awareness emerges from the reactions of group members toward one another as they explore the implications of their behavior.

4. An ICW is not as intensive or emotionally personalized as a T-group.

Ingram (1975), a foreign student advisor at the University of Washington, further differentiates the ICW from sensitivity training groups in their purposes, methods, and dynamics. The ICW increases awareness of cultural influences on human values and behavior, whereas the sensitivity training group tries to bring about personal change in the individual's behavior. The ICW is structured with an agenda focused on subjects for discussion on cultural differences both in the "there and then" *and* the "here and now," with norms set by the trainer. The sensitivity training group, however, tends to be unstructured, with less attention to the subject under discussion and more emphasis on the "here-and-now" process going on in the group, with norms set by the group. Consequently, the ICW tends to be less intense than the sensitivity training group. The ICW devotes more attention to cultural and less attention to personal aspects of behavior. Trainees are taught about their own culture and how that culture differs from other cultures. They learn the extent to which these differences can cause problems in communicating with members of different ethnic groups. As Trainees become aware of their own culture and/or subculture, the extent to which this interferes with their ability to interact with others, they are better able to accept the importance of individual and cultural differences and the influence of stereotypes, preconceptions, value judgments, and anxiety.

The achievement of competencies mentioned in the previous section have best been achieved in small groups that are themselves composed of persons from different cultures. A number of ICWs have been designed to change attitudes and behaviors toward improved human relations. Clarke (1972), Hull (1972), Silverthorne and Goldberg (1972), and Barndt (1972) have led small intercultural workshop groups and published materials describing their goals and outcomes. There is a similarity among these workshop designs that highlights some particularly important objectives.

First, each training method emphasized the importance of achieving an awareness of cultural differences in terms of values, customs, and rules that affect human relations. The small group itself is a useful resource to identify significant aspects of the participants own culture, to become aware of alternative cultural systems, and to generate from small group experiences to the pluralist outside world.

Second, there is an emphasis on understanding the effects of cultural differences as manifested in the behavior of the participants, the other group members, and persons outside the group. Participants are better able to understand particular, unique, and specific values when they approach different cultures. Some understanding of needs fulfilled by cultural bias is the beginning of an attempt to replace that bias with alternative attitudes.

Third, participants are taught to listen carefully to the other person's thought, words, and actions as they are expressed both verbally and nonverbally. Although these groups are carefully distinguished from sensitivity training groups, participants do expect to emerge with increased skills in being sensitive to the needs of persons from other cultures. The process of communication describes one important focus of the intercultural group design, with special attention to the ways in which cultural differences inhibit those communications.

Fourth, appreciation of the values held by others without at the same time rejecting one's own values is an important aspect of the design. Each participant goes through a process of awareness and evaluation that applies both to her own culture and the culture of others in the group. She develops criteria distinguishing between aspects of other cultures that can be accepted and those that must be rejected, without having to reject persons holding those values. There is a significant difference between disagreeing with another person's beliefs and forcing one's own beliefs on that person as the single criterion of truth.

Fifth, the ability to interact in a context of support and trust in spite of difference is a goal that depends on the achievement of all previous goals. There is an elusive quality of fellowship that defies accurate measurement, but which ranks high on any list of intercultural goals. It is achieved more often as a by-product of the "successful" group than through any deliberate plan or method. More than any other accomplishment, it characterizes the strength of a group and the value of interaction to participants.

The Case Study Simulation

The case study has been used traditionally in training for law and medicine, and more recently for development for intercultural training. The case typically consists of a problem situation presented from the perspective of one point of view. The trainee may be required to generate and assume additional information from limited facts and incomplete background. The case study has been used for training in specific skills or in dealing with the problems of a specific population area. The trainee participates vicariously from the point of view of the case narrator, who presents the information.

The style and type of case study used are the primary influence on whether the learning situation will be effective. The emphasis is on the learning situation as the objective rather than the technique or device used, with the ultimate goal being increased knowledge or changed behaviors of the trainee. There are numerous styles of case studies. The "vignette" mode presents a problem situation in a brief description attempting to illustrate specific concepts of interaction. The study is incomplete in that it merely presents the stimuli, relying on the trainer's skill to apply anticipated and unanticipated insights as they arise. Trainees should have the opportunity to evaluate as well as assist in presenting the case study. They may choose to role-play aspects of the problem to better empathize with the conditions of that situation.

A stimulating case study can create a motivation and desire for more learning about that particular situation or skill, allowing the trainee to escape *into* reality. Each particular situation or incident has a learning potential as one component. Trainees are then involved in exploring underlying concepts as those concepts are embodied in the experiences of others. The active case study as described by Kleitsch (1971) has five components.

1. Development and/or selection of an event, in which the criteria of selection or case presentation are problem dimensions with a sequential organization and/or principles to be learned.

2. Fabrication or modification of the problem so that the learner is provided only the basic problem statement, with the requirement that the alternatives and solution are to be devised by the learner.

3. Recognition that the case has an historical precedent and that the principle or case precedent is the "thing" to be learned, not necessarily the specific data or content comprising the case in point.

4. Discussion of the alternatives with a controlled focus on just the case in point, with later extrapolation to other events and interpretation provided in instructional form.

5. Validation of a solution based on its approximation to what actually happened, plus testing of mastery of case study principles through transfer to kindred cases.

The "Active Case Study" method designed by Kleitsch at Instructional Simulations, Inc., applies the case method to a variety of other modes. It begins by looking at the concept to be explored and its social application. As an example, consider the concept of autocracy and imagine the various ways that particular concept can be behavioralized for learning. The concept is presented in the case study through a process or method that demonstrates how that concept is linked to other concepts. The trainee is then provided with an identity, resources, alternative points of view, local customs and norms, an internal operating procedure, problem components that may give different information to different participants in the case study, alternatives to the problems, and a notion of reward or pay-off.

Behaviors become the means for presenting each case study in a sociodrama setting. The information component of each study is limited to carefully prescribed parameters, yet the information is distributed among participants in such a way that each must rely on one another to make conclusions or to solve problems (Aronson, 1975). Some examples of active case studies might include moot court, mock legislatures, planning a business, planning a new product, adopting an ideology, mock political conventions, devising a career, an international dispute, building a town, planning a family, or preventing a war.

The active case study blends various methods to focus on activities required by the learner to deal with the actual situation or skill that defines the training goal. The active case study provides a focus and a climactic episode or goal for the training process. The trainee is oriented toward the application of those training goals in specific events.

Packaged programs using simulation techniques are increasingly popular, although the real learning in training results from a group having to design its own unique simulation exercise according to its needs and resources. The shortage of trainers and the increased numbers of trainees suggest that simulation packages will continue to supply the training mode for a large portion of programs. The incorporation of real incidents and increased popularity of "on-site" training can be seen as an extension of the simulation model to the whole target environment as a training workshop.

As outlined by Alger (in Guetzkow, 1963), games (1) heighten the interest and motivation of students as an enjoyable class experience, (2) offer opportunities to apply and to test knowledge in friendly competition which (3) provides greater understanding of practical applications in applied knowledge through (4) a miniature society or world in a controlled lab setting.

The traditional educational system contains structural defects that are avoided in games. (1) Students are traditionally taught for a future environment, but their priorities of concern are frequently limited to the more immediate present. (2) The system is partially (if not entirely) limited to enforced, involuntary, routinized activities which do not allow for voluntary action or regard spectacular achievement except, perhaps, in extra-mural activities. (3) The teacher in this system is forced to assume conflicting roles as "teacher" and "judge," thus incurring hostility, servility, alienation, or reaction by students to this "authority figure." Games, on the other hand, (1) bring the future into the present, (2) rely on self-discipline and inspire high motivation, and (3) allow evaluation and judgment of success or failure that are largely self-imposed.

The use of games in simulated environments has been explored in management training and in aspects of the socio-economic environment, international relations, political decision making, and in-teacher training. In Asia, the Management Institute for Training and Research in Asia (MITRA) has developed numerous simulation exercises appropriate to the Asian environment. Research in evaluating and measuring the outcome of game theory, although just being started, indicates the usefulness of this approach as compared to more traditional models.

A number of criticisms have been directed toward game theory as a useful research or teaching approach (Shubik, 1964). (1) Do individuals have a preference system fixed through time? (2) How are preferences for uncertain events obtained? (3) Is an individual's preference system measurable? (4) Are values comparable between different decision makers? (5) Is "utility" transferable between decision-makers? (6) Are individual preferences tentative; that is, if a is preferred to b and b is preferred to c, does this imply that a is preferred to c? (7) Do individuals misperceive the value of certain outcomes? (8) What is the fineness in variation an individual may perceive with respect to slightly different outcomes? (9) Are there gaps in an individual's knowledge of outcomes? (10) Are there gaps in an individual's knowledge of the alternatives available to him? (11) Does an individual's value for an outcome depend on the value of the outcome to others than himself? (12) Can there be social values independent of individual values? (13) Can a consistent social preference system be constructed from an aggregation of individual preferences? Cross-cultural training programs that use a simulation can benefit by the participant's examining these questions.

Simulation training promises international and intercultural collaboration to better understand and deal appropriately with cultural differences. Numerous specialized simulation training packages such as the Culture Assimilator and the Contrast American, (both covered elsewhere in this book) have structured specific combinations of simulated interaction to provide a basis for research, as well as increased cooperation to identify both the cultural universals and unique aspects of participating cultures.

Additional materials on how to design simulations and on international or intercultural simulations in distribution are listed in Greenblat (1972), who cites hundreds of articles and resources. Weeks, Pedersen, and Brislin (1975) have prepared a handbook of simulations and structured exercises, particularly on intercultural learning, from the less readily and previously "fugitive" materials being used. Simon, Howe, and Kirchenbaum (1972) are particularly good in presenting material on practical strategies for "values clarification" in a course or program.

The Cross-Cultural Coalition Training Model

There is an increasing need for a model to train mental health professionals to work in multicultural populations. Citing evidence of institutional racism in the traditional selection, training, and certification methods of mental health professionals, Vontress (1969) calls for more in-service and preservice training designed to help counselors examine their attitudes toward the culturally different by exposing the counselors directly to the culture of their clients. There is increasing evidence from professional psychologists that trained counselors are not prepared to deal with individuals who come from different racial, ethnic, or socioeconomic groups whose values, attitudes, and general life styles are different from their own (Torrey, 1971; Padilla, Boxley, and Wagner, 1972; Pedersen, 1974; Pedersen et al., 1975).

To be an effective counselor it is important to understand clients in their cultural context. The most promising training model in counselor education for accomplishing that task is *microcounseling* or looking at a counselor's specific behaviors in a simulated interview setting with videotaped feedback. This approach encourages orientations, bridging the gap between classroom learning and initial applied experiences of actual counseling (Ivey, 1971).

The model, as described by Ivey and Gluckstern (1974), involves nine basic steps (1) The trainee is first matched with a coached client. (2) The trainee interviews the client while being videotaped. (3) The client evaluates the interview. (4) The trainee discusses specific target skills with the supervisor. (5) The trainee views videotaped models of those specific skills. (6) The trainee critiques her own videotaped interview. (7) The supervisor and trainee review target skills and plan for the next season. (8) The trainee reinterviews the same client. (9) Feedback and evaluation of the final session are discussed with the supervisor. In a modification of this model, Guttman and Haase (1972) suggest a microinteraction approach that would (1) identify client behaviors consistent with a positive outcome of counseling, (2) identify counselor behaviors that lead to those client behaviors, and (3) implement a behavioral training model in which the counselor's acquisition of skills is contingent on consultation with the client, rather than from a supervisor.

Most applications of microcounseling utilize some form of recording such as videotape for self-confrontation by the trainee (see treatment of this technique, pp. 108–109). Kagan (1969) has effectively demonstrated that videotapes of a trainee's counseling session can help to identify and strengthen positive facilitative behaviors and change nonfacilitative behaviors, using the supervisor as a third person who interrogates and debriefs the trainee after the interview. Reivich and Geertsma (1969) have reviewed the literature dealing with observational media used in training therapists, such as videotaped demonstrations of desired behaviors and self-observation by the trainee, including videotapes as the focal point of supervisory sessions.

Counseling can be described as a function of push-and-pull factors in which the counselor seeks fulfillment in being helpful, and the client seeks to reconcile internalized ambiguity. Counseling, viewed as an active rather than a passive entity, seeks its own survival and increased power over the client. In cross-cultural counseling, this can result in a triad of stress, response to it, and ameliorative intervention, all three of which are potentially subject to being culturally mediated (Draguns and Phillips, 1972). Bolman (1968) suggested that at least two therapists, one representing each culture, be used in cross-cultural therapy to provide a bridge between the population being served and the counselor. In this way counseling can both transcend the ethnocentric approach and incorporate the contributions of each culture to the relationship through mutual adaptation.

The cross-cultural coalition training model places three persons in a videotaped microcounseling context to role-play a simulated critical incident problem of cross-cultural counseling. In this modification of the microcounseling model, developed by Pedersen (1973), the counselor role is filled by a counselor trainee matched with two persons, one in the client role and one in an anticounselor or problem role. This paired team is from the same culture, but it must be a culture different from the counselor's culture. The three-way interaction of counselor, client, and anticounselor is expected to explicate cultural aspects of the problem and resistance to counseling in an open struggle for power between the counselor and the anticounselor more effectively than can be accomplished in a cross-cultural counseling dyad model.

The unique element in this modification is the personified and personalized role of the anticounselor. The anticounselor is encouraged to think that his best interest is preventing the counselor from coalesing with the client toward a "solution" of the problem. Generally, the anticounselor, seeking to increase the client's dependence on the problem, attempts to achieve goals opposite from those of the counselor. The person in the counselor role is encouraged to build an effective helping relationship with the client that will weaken or diminish the problem's influence on the client. Generally, the counselors are encouraged to deal with the client much as they would in a normal counselor-client dyad. The person in the client role is encouraged to accept help or guidance from both the counselor and the anticounselor according to which of these two persons seems to offer a more satisfactory alliance. The client is then forced to choose between the counselor from another culture or the anticounselor from his own culture.

This design assumes that counseling occurs in a force field in which the counselor, client, and the problem interact in a constellation of conflicting or complementary goals. Counseling is thus conceptualized as a dynamic interaction of contrary forces in the mode of social power theory; either an equilibrium is achieved between the counselor and the client, on the one hand, or the problem creates resistance to counseling and increased disequilibrium, thereby isolating the client from alternative sources of help. The distribution and use of power in counseling properly encourages a temporary means-oriented alliance between counselor and client as an alternative to the client's continued and indeterminate dependence on the problem. A counselor-client coalition against the problem becomes the vehicle of effective counseling, whereas ineffective counseling results in a client-problem coalition that isolates the counselor.

The triad training model offers numerous advantages that complement previously discussed training models which, although not yet supported with research evidence, suggest an accommodation between counseling technique and cross-cultural training. The counselor and her client from a different culture are able to interact in the safety of a simulated interview to accomplish the specific and limited goal of teaching one another about implications cultural values have in counseling. In that setting negative feedback can be encouraged through the anticounselor's role, with a minimum threat to counselor trainees. Trainees are able to see the power balance between themselves and clients change in specific, concrete ways. The diffuse and abstract nature of resistance often associated with working among clients from other cultures is avoided. As the counselor makes mistakes she is corrected immediately, even in the midst of making the mistake, and can view her mistakes on videotape. Trainees can be made aware of their own bias that might otherwise interfere with actual counseling; they can learn about their own counseling effectiveness from persons in the target culture itself. Clients are given a meaningful role in training counselors for work among "their" people in an exchange for knowledge authentic to healthy interpersonal relationships.

Perhaps the most difficult role to conceptualize is that of the anticounselor. Although the strategies of a counselor and the role expectations of a client are familiar to us, the notion of an active, back-talking person. at first seems bizzare and strange. The anticounselor role develops its own unique strategies. In many ways the anticounselor has more to lose than either the counselor or the client, because his very existence is at stake.

The role of the anticounselor as a problem is distinguished from the role of a person *with* a problem. Having a partner from his or her same culture to challenge the counselor provides a valuable source of negative feedback. The role of the client is, consequently, strengthened as the sought-out partner for a winning coalition with either of the other two participants. In preliminary trials, otherwise passive counselor trainees become noticeably more agressive when faced with a third person in the role of an anticounselor. Persons who try the role of anticounselor find it difficult at first to empathize with the problem, having associated the problem exclusively with the "enemy" of a counseling relationship. As trainees became more familiar with the problem role, they are able to build on those more attractive and tempting resources offered by an "unresolved" problem. The anticounselor trainee uses many counseling skills and cultural insights working toward the opposite direction from the position he might take as a counselor. The anticounselor role further offers hueristic value by providing a "back door" to understanding the counseling process. Some of the following problem strategies, taken from actual experience with the technique, bring out overt examples of symbolic or otherwise hidden sources of resistance to counseling which would predictably be *intensified* by cultural barriers.

The anticounselor can reinforce the benefits a "problem" offers and the dangers implicit in seeking counseling from an outsider, keeping the interaction on a superficial level, sidetracking the counselor away from a client's *real* concerns, getting in between the counselor and client to confuse or distort communication and bring out a counselor's defensiveness. Anticounselors need not be consistent or open in their tactics. They can easily whisper or use a language unfamiliar to the counselor in communicating with the client, attempting to exclude the counselor in any way possible. Anticounselors can further mislead the counselor or distract the counselor away from the client, even by emphasizing the extreme importance of "cultural" differences themselves, challenging the counselor to come up with an instant solution and intensifying whatever negative feedback perceived in the client. Anticounselors can redirect "blame" toward some scapegoat or impossible complication, pointing out the weaknesses in whatever the counselor suggests and playing on a client's indecision to keep counseling at an obscure and general level. Anticounselors can discredit the counselor, demanding credentials or the definition of terms, pointing out the importance of finding a counselor from the client's own culture, and preventing any purposive change from happening as a result of the interview.

The cross-cultural coalition model uses videotaped simulation of cross-cultural counseling interviews between a client, the counselor, and an anticounselor. It attempts to identify the problem more clearly from the client-culture point of view by allowing an anticounselor from one culture to empathize with and rehearse the kinds of specific resistance a counselor from another culture is likely to encounter when dealing with a client from the anticounselor's culture.

If the cross-cultural coalition model demonstrates its effectiveness in training counselors, it might supplement traditional training in a variety of ways. Nonspecialist counselors and paraprofessionals in training are being sought out for advice or help but, lacking formal training in counseling, are frequently more dependent on self-taught skills. Even without benefit of understanding the theories of counselor training, the cross-cultural coalition model reinforces those behaviors that produce a counselor-client coalition and punishes behaviors that destroy that coalition. As a supplement to traditional curricula in formal counselor education, the model provides a useful link between didactic theory and practicum experiences in cross-cultural counseling. The model is directed toward both formal classes of preservice training and in-service training programs among persons already working in multicultural populations.

Facilitator Development Institutes

The Center for Cross-Cultural Communication, branching out from the Facilitator Development Institute in Holland under the direction of Charles Devonshire, has organized a series of workshops in Europe. The approach is different from other approaches we have discussed in their emphasis on training facilitators. The center's approach is based on principles of humanistic psychology and draws heavily on small-group techniques popular in the United States. Although there is considerable interest in Europe for learning about small-group experiences being developed in the United States, most universities in Europe, or even in the United States, do not offer programs in their curriculum designed to train *facilitators,* or leaders of small groups.

The Facilitator Development Institute is an attempt to impose some quality controls on the out-of-university training for facilitators, recognizing that many self-styled facilitators are posing as experts in the field without benefit of training. The facilitator development program combines experiential and cognitive elements at the Institute in Holland and more recently at workshops in Germany, Sweden, and Great Britain. Carl Rogers, a consultant to the Center for Cross-Cultural Communication, describes the program's benefits as broadly based (in Devonshire, 1975, p. 1).

"It usually consists of ten to fifteen persons and a facilitator or leader. It is relatively unstructured, providing a climate of maximum freedom for personal expression, exploration of feelings and interpersonal communication. Emphasis is upon the interaction among group members, in an atmosphere which encourages each to drop his defenses and facades and thus enables him to relate directly and openly to other members of the group. Individuals come to know themselves and each other more fully than is possible in the usual social or working relationship; the climate of openness, risk-taking and honesty generates trust, which enables the person to recognize and change self-defeating attitudes, test out and adopt more innovative and constructive behaviors, and subsequently to relate more adequately and efficiently to others in his every day life."

The workshops are rooted in principles of humanistic psychology, but behavioristic approaches in a range of techniques such as person-centered styles, Gestalt, meditation, role playing, psychodrama and a variety of other approaches are included, without advocating that any particular approach is most suitable for all participants. During the last two summers the program has attracted educators, social workers, psychologists and psychiatrists, graduate students, industrial consultants, military personnel, volunteers, professors, sociologists, anthropologists, church workers, researchers, and a wide variety of other persons interested in exchanging knowledge about small-group training approaches.

Aside from the professional staff of the institute, facilitators are chosen from among the participants in previous years to ensure a variety of viewpoints in the institute and to give leadership roles to participants. Although there are many models and designs for organizing small groups, there are few models for training facilitators of small groups. The skills required for a small intercultural group are even more specialized and demanding. There is a need for hard data comparing aspects of the various training designs and measuring their effectiveness in training facilitators from a variety of viewpoints.

The National Training Laboratory (NTL) T Group Model

The National Training Laboratory (NTL) approach is widely associated with encounter groups and was an early leader in sensitivity training groups in Bethel, Maine. Unfortunately, they have not applied their resources to the specific problems of international or cross-cultural orientation. There has been some interest by NTL in producing materials for cross-cultural orientation, but to date the only significant publication has been the book by Nylen (1967) on staff training materials developed for use in Africa. Although this handbook has made a significant contribution and is widely used in programs of cross-cultural orientation, its most important portion are the several hundred pages of exercises adapted for cross-cultural orientation. Most of these exercises are already well known to persons organizing cross-cultural orientation programs, and many of them have proven their value to those of us that have used them.

The first hundred pages of Nylen and Mitchell (1967) makes some attempt to adapt the standard approaches of small group training to the international/intercultural population. The materials systematically look at the individual, group systems, role perceptions, role functions, communication, frustration, performance and growth, leadership, change, and the helping relationship. One of the difficulties in transferring the NTL training group model to the international or intercultural population is that the T group model is so very "American" in its approach. Many of the very values spoken of earlier that define the American approach to direct confrontation, instant sharing and openness of feelings, majority rules, and physical contact in friendship are even more evident in T-groups and consequently even more offensive outside a fairly narrow culturally defined population. In some ways the American response to sensitivity training and encounter groups resembles a religious conviction even though, to follow that analogy, missionaries of that viewpoint have not been very successful outside the upper-middle-class urban American culture.

Multinational Corporation Training Programs

There are close to a million American businessmen and their families living abroad, and probably two hundred thousand of them are actually engaged in business. Surprisingly, there are few formal systems or rigid procedures that guide the development of international executives. Chorafas (1967) surveyed international firms to discover their plans for domestic personnel training. Until about 1960 (Trail, 1968) the design and initiation of technical assistance training programs was sporadic and haphazard, with no systematic attempt to determine what areas of understanding and skill were necessary to ensure the successful performance of international personnel. Barrett and Bass (1972), after visiting forty countries in a survey of training methods, strongly suggested that the utility of any given training method is strongly dependent on the cultural setting. In more "traditional" societies, more directive, lecture approaches are expected and successful for training, whereas in the more "advanced" societies participative approaches were most favored and accepted.

In the past, there were two types of technical assistance programs. In the turnkey approach a company or country builds an entire factory or technical complex in a developing country, establishes the factory's working procedures, uses its own staff to operate the factory, trains nationals to fill all the occupational roles in the factory, and when the nationals are adequately trained the foreign company or country turns over the key and leaves. The other type of approach involves training of individuals, one by one, for specific jobs or assignments abroad. The task of selecting and then training technical experts, usually without adequate lead time, has not proven to be entirely successful, as Asher (1962) pointed out:

> "Our ignorance regarding the personal qualities needed by instigators of social change is even greater. The preparation of laundry lists of desirable qualities has become a favorite occupation, but, alas, all that emerges is an ideal man who does not exist. We do not know how to create him, and we might not recognize him if we saw him. He must be cultured

and cross-cultured. He must be disciplined and interdisciplined. He must be well stocked with empathy and antifreeze. He must be a model himself, and he must know about model-building, institution building and body building."

To determine the basic curriculum divisions and subject matter areas in the training programs for international technical assistants Trail (1968) examined the program syllabi of 150 training programs and reviewed training reports written by specialists in the field of technical assistance. Three major curriculum areas were characteristic of the 115 training programs examined. These were (1) professional and technical considerations, (2) cross-cultural understanding and (3) developmental processes. Trail examined the training priorities set by business, government, religious, university, and voluntary agencies. Both traditional and experimental types of training programs devoted 60 to 70 percent of training time to technician orientation in the areas of agency objectives and administrative considerations. All agencies except the university programs included knowing about the "home office" in the United States as an important aspect. The university programs did not emphasize technical and professional training, assuming perhaps that graduates would receive such orientation after they were employed by a technical assistance agency.

Cross-cultural orientation is recognized as one of the more important training divisions and as a prerequisite for effective overseas performance. Technicians must be able to relate and utilize their skills abroad for them to be useful. The majority of training program directors, however, indicated that only about 10 to 25 percent of orientation time was allocated to cross-cultural understanding. Within cross-cultural orientation programs the emphasis has been on cultural adjustment, language skills, and history of the culture of the host country.

Analyzing the division of developmental processes has been recognized as important by cross-cultural specialists, but is perhaps the least well known to trainers of the three curricula areas. Only about one-quarter of the agencies spent time in this area, which seldom exceeded 10 percent of the training time. The government and university agencies have emphasized the importance of developmental processes perhaps more than other agencies. The assumption is apparently that developmental processes can best be learned by the technician in the overseas environment, although there is no evidence that this, in fact, occurs.

Some of the more general problem areas encountered by American businessmen abroad include difficulty in coping with the rules of the host society, adjusting to the geography and climate of the new location, being outside the mainstream of life in the host culture, and experiencing the loneliness of culture shock. To be more specific, problems arise within the business or organization; examples are working with the legal or political regulations of the host country, following international laws and regulations relative to the business, being understood by the home office, and keeping all family members happy in a strange culture. If the multinational corporation wants to use local nationals in the business, they face problems of finding a capable manager with enough of the right kind of educational or technological background who can deal with local attitudes hostile to multinational corporations from developed countries, have different ideas about what constitutes good management, and resist following the operational rules the corporation might require from its home office.

In order for a multinational corporation to train its own personnel for assignment abroad, certain requirements must be observed. First of all, the trainee must be given a period of time to prepare before going and to make the transition between his job back home and abroad. Second, the training should be conducted in a location with persons from cultures other than the trainees and as close to the future host culture as possible. The cultural differences themselves provide opportunities to increase a trainees' awareness of cultural differences between themselves and others. Third, the transition training period should involve both the trainee and his or her family as a unit. Fourth, the transition training program should include some language study. Fifth, the training design should focus on problems or skills specifically relevant to the trainee's future job.

There are a number of reasons why a comprehensive

training program such as that outlined above might not be used. One immediate reason is the cost of training an individual and his family, both in terms of lost work time and support during training. Another related constraint is the time involved in training, which assumes that people are selected long before they actually leave and that they can be spared from their job for the training period. Finally, there is no completely satisfactory way of guaranteeing that the training will pay off in terms of dollars and cents for the corporation. It is hard to measure changes resulting from training, and harder still to put a price tag on those changes.

There are a number of institutions that have specialized in training multinational corporation personnel. Some of the training programs mentioned elsewhere in this book include businessmen as trainees. The Thunderbird Graduate School of International Management is perhaps the best known organization in the United States. Most of the larger universities are developing programs in multinational business practices also.

Roles as Cultures

Societies have taught us to be culturally different from one another through role expectations that define the limits of our freedom. In subtle ways we are taught who we are and which values or assumptions make "us" uniquely different from "them." As the world's cultures are becoming increasingly integrated and as we are required to assume multiple roles, the concept "cross-cultural" begins to lose its meaning and becomes simply a dimension of all interpersonal relationships. To the extent that our roles resemble cultures, each of us belongs to many "cultures" at the same time. The final and most impressive impact of cross-cultural orientation might, therefore, be in the area of interpersonal relationships, helping us accommodate the different roles and values of persons within our own nationality and ethnic group.

The example of sex role provides us with a clear illustration of ways in which roles resemble cultures. In many respects the problems of sexism resemble problems of racism, especially in its effects on human relationships. The prejudged expectations for persons on that other role are more important in our evaluation than the data of our first-hand experiences. The Emma Willard Task Force on Education provides the best example we know of to attempt to train persons toward a better understanding of sexism as it affects our point of view. This section attempts to present a brief example of ways in which persons in a variety of roles, such as sex roles, might provide the largest audience for cross-cultural training.

The Emma Willard Task Force (1972) suggests 14 criteria for evaluating materials to determine the presence of a sexist bias in human relations curriculum. These criteria provide a basis for evaluation on many other roles as well. (1) Does the sexism component of the human relations program deal with personal, cultural, and institutional sexism? Is it oriented toward both awareness and action? (2) Do the people conducting the human relations courses (including any consultants brought in for portions of the course) have nonsexist attitudes? (3) Did community input include women who see sexism as a problem? (4) Does the sexism component have both cognitive and affective experiences? (5) Does the program give concrete information on the current status of women? (6) Does it show the socialization process from birth to adulthood and show how all facets of society contribute sex-role stereotyping? (7) Does it show how sexism pervades the school system? Does this include student-related issues (e.g., books and materials, courses, extracurricular activities, academic and vocational counseling, and teacher and counselor attitudes)? Does this include employment-related issues (e.g., housewives, mothers, workers, AFDC mothers, volunteers, students, single women, married women, divorced women, gay women, elderly women, prisoners, alcoholics, women from all racial and ethnic backgrounds)? (9) Does it show the relationship of sexism to other problems of our society (racism, poverty, militarism, etc.)? (10) Does it relate women's liberation to men's liberation? (11) Does it provide feminist resources (including the Emma Willard Task Force on Education)? (12) Does it help participants explore what they can do, both in their personal life and in their schools? (13) What is the long-range focus?

(The long-range goal is to eliminate sexism from the schools, at which time there would not have to be women's issues, history, etc., compartmentalized into special courses; the concerns will have been incorporated into the school curriculum administrative rules, etc.) (14) Does the school's human relations support system include sexism as a significant concern?

The sex-role bias, like other prejudices, is evident in our language. The generic use of such words as man, mankind, manpower, forefathers, brotherhood, chairman implicitly orient us toward a particular point of view in spite of ourselves. Look at the advertisements in popular mass media and notice how closely sex roles are linked to particular tasks, professions, and life styles that are completely unrelated in any functional way to the person's sex. Note particularly that the women are all pretty, the children are all healthy, and the men are all handsome. Our advertisements, perhaps more than any other part of the media, reflect back to us and train us to accept the popular images of our role.

The materials used in education are one of the most effective measures of how we socialize ourselves in a particular role/cultural bias. In a survey of 144 elementary readers from 15 major series, the Wildner materials show that 900 stories had a boy as the main character, but only 344 stories had a girl as the main character. Boys were portrayed as active and independent, girls as passive and fearful. Women were referred to only as "Mother" 69 percent of the time, usually pictured through a kitchen window in the illustrations. Although there were 131 biographies of famous men, there were only 23 biographies of famous women. The difference between men and women is clearly hierarchical, without equitable access to power, as described in each of the systems we use to teach about ourselves. A simple test of that statement would be to role-play a situation with reversed roles, that is, men taking the role of women and women taking the role of men, through one of the many simulated exercises recently available. The Emma Willard Task Force has published a 30-page bibliography of materials, films, books, simulations, and educational resources illustrating various aspects of sexism in education.

Additional training materials are available through the

Federal Women's program, U.S. Civil Service Commission Room 7530, 1900 E. Street, N.W. Washington, D.C. 20415. They have organized a network of consultant resources, and development of awareness materials is being formed by the Women's Caucus of the American Society for Training and Development. Loring and Wells (1972) provides some valuable materials on training women in business. Other groups, such as the Women's Action Alliance 370 Lexington Avenue, New York, N.Y. 10017, are trying to translate the growing awareness of sex discrimination into concrete proposals. These groups have focused on the subtle training and orientation that is *already* occurring in our advertising, our school curriculum, and throughout the media through an implicit bias rooted in our own cultural values. The task of orientation, then, is largely remedial, to counteract the bias we have already been taught without perhaps knowing it.

As we become more aware of our membership in special populations relating to sex, age, life style, and social role, we can see more clearly how these groups function much as cultures, with their own expectations defining our behaviors. The function of an orientation program is to increase our awareness of the ways our roles have been defined by others and thereby to increase our freedom in defining our own roles in society.

We predict that the increased awareness of special populations that was brought forth in the 1960s and early 1970s will continue in importance and will not be a passing fancy that causes attention but then dwindles away from public view. A basic knowledge of these concerns is a prerequisite to effective functioning in everyday life.

The Reinforcement-Behavioral Model of Training

David (1972) applied the principles of reinforcement to reduce and prevent adjustment problems by prescribing changes in three different areas. (1) Learning the stimulus cues that are necessary to attain reinforcers and to avoid punishers, (2) Transferring and modifying present reinforcing systems or developing new reinforcers and (3) Changing, neutralizing, and avoiding punishers. Identifying the basic elements for this approach involves learning appropriate behaviors—things a person may or may not do—in the target culture, learning the strategies and techniques used in recognizing those cues, and being skilled in applying these insights through one's own behavior.

The first step is being aware of the connection between a stimulus cue experience and an appropriate response. Before departure to the target culture, trainees will not be able to learn all the stimulus cues of that culture. Rather, they are limited to those stimuli most predictably connected with their work, task, or purpose in that target culture. For example, learning how their hosts express approval and disapproval will help them to understand their system of dispensing rewards and punishments. The trainee's success will depend on his appropriate discrimination between and response to these cues.

David (1972) suggested a systematic attempt to employ reinforcers through trainee's answers to four clusters of questions. (1) What are your major sources of reinforcement back home? What do you do that you enjoy doing most? (2) Are there events that might occur but have not yet happened which would act as potential reinforcers? Is there anything that you hope might happen? (3) How many of these present and potential reinforcers are available in the host culture? What are the things you hope will happen after you arrive? (4) Which events in the host culture can be used as reinforcers during predeparture training? How can we anticipate the good things that might happen and rehearse your experiencing them?

After the sources of a trainee's reinforcement have been established, the next step is to determine how many of those sources will be available in the host culture. Some of the reinforcers will be available, some will not, some may or may not be anticipated according to the accuracy of the information about the host culture. Some reinforcers, such as reading the morning paper, can be made available with some extra effort. Some reinforcers, like American food, might be available but with reduced quality, frequency, and variety. The individual training program is then developed in cooperation with the trainee to identify, modify, and apply as many of the previously enjoyed reinforcers as possible.

Identifying punishers in the host culture follows the same process structure, through responses to a series of questions. (1) What events are punishing back home? What do you most dislike doing? (2) What events have a potential punishing effect? What sorts of things might happen that would be unpleasant? (3) Which of these punishing events are apt to be experienced in the host culture? What are the bad things that are likely to happen in the target culture? What have others going to those cultures found most disagreeable? How many of these punishers can be modified, changed, or eliminated? How many of these disagreeable experiences can be avoided?

Each person will differ somewhat from the others in what he or she finds to be most disagreeable or punishing, which means that a program must be tailored to the individual needs of each trainee. The trainee might then have the opportunity to rehearse some of the events he/she expects to be most punishing through simulated interaction, and to anticipate the response to the alternative possibilities which are available.

Through training, the punishers can be modified or might even be changed to reinforcers, like learning to enjoy the food of the target culture and some of the previously unfamiliar parts of the daily routine. Minimally, the negative effect of punishers can be reduced or neutralized as the trainee learns to respond appropriately. The trainee may learn new skills to cope with the punishers and to avoid events that are likely to result in punishment.

David (1972) suggested several methods, based on social learning theory, for training sojourners to adjust to another culture. The training requires participation of persons knowledgeable in social learning theory and skilled in application of theoretical insights, backed up by a trained staff with access to accurate and precise information about the culture and the reinforcers or punishers appropriate to each trainee. Bandura (1969) related social learning theory to training programs. R. Campbell's (1969) review of personnel training and development included a social learning theory training model. The process incorporates three social learning procedures.

(1) Modeling the requisite behaviors for interacting with the host culture can be done before departure. The trainee can learn and practice the necessary behaviors modeled on the behaviors of host nationals or returnees thought to have been successful in the host culture, under simulated conditions until they are performed correctly. The models provide insight into stimulus cues which can then be learned by the trainee. This does not mean learning to imitate every aspect of the host national or returnee, but to select and modify those cues appropriate to the trainee's role, function, and opportunities as sojourners.

(2) The simulation of host culture conditions, used in much of the Peace Corps training, required establishing a small model of the host culture in the training setting. Unless the simulation is carefully structured with clearly defined and accepted goals, the simulation is of limited value. Without such an understanding of these goals, trainees are likely to view such simulations as artificial and irrelevant. A good simulation familiarizes the trainees with the host culture environment and allows them to develop new reinforcers in anticipation of the foreign experience. They are able to adjust to the strangeness of the host culture under controlled conditions that can provide clues to additional training needs.

(3) Aversive events in the host culture can result in fear-reactions or inappropriate avoidance by the trainee. The process of desensitization and counterconditioning allows the trainee to experience the fearful stimulus cue and understand his or her response more fully. The trainee is asked to imagine the feared event, such as being ridiculed by the hosts for errors in language. First, the trainee is asked to imagine such a process of ridicule actually taking place. Second, the strength of aversive stimuli is increased gradually from imagining using the host language with nobody around, up to the point where the trainee imagines making the most serious error among host nationals who ridicule public attempts at their language. During this procedure the trainee is presented with a reinforcer immediately following the aversive stimulus such as muscular relaxation or imagining pleasurable experiences.

The two sets of experiences are alternated, with the effect of reducing the fear-reaction of the trainee to specific aspects of the host culture.

Analysis of the host culture in terms of the precise concepts of learning-reinforcement theory allows training to be very explicit with the trainer focusing on concrete problems. We have found that the approach is very rarely used, probably because of the negative connotations associated with reinforcement principles and psychological control, but rejection for these reasons is unfortunate. The application of learning theory can often help identify problems of adjustment in cross-cultural orientation more accurately than other, less-precise approaches. Trainers should be encouraged to include some aspect of this approach in their own identification of problems for cross-cultural adjustment.

3

REVIEWS OF PROGRAMS

With the content of chapter 2 as a background, we would now like to review a number of cross-cultural orientation programs that have been put into practice.

The Army's Alien Presence

The field of cross-cultural training can benefit from the frequently neglected research in this area by the military. Since 1964 the Army research office has sponsored a cross-cultural training program developed by the American Institutes for Research (AIR). The program has trained large numbers of U.S. Army troops in the Far East, largely in Thailand and Korea. In the latter country, parallel programs exist for both United States and South Korean personnel. Information about the program was derived from the writings of Humphrey (1964; 1968), Spector (1968; 1969), Spector, Parris, Humphrey, Aronson, and Williams (1969), and from conversations with AIR officials. In addition, an unpublished summary of the program written by Dr. Bert King (Summarized in R. Campbell, 1969) was helpful.

Content of program and trainees. The very reasonable goals, which also provide the framework for the program, are presented at the beginning of Chapter one. These goals are based on the ideology that there is a fundamental goodness in human beings, and that this ideal can be communicated to United States troops. The content of the program consists of briefings, discussions, and an action program. Examples will be for Korea, because a large amount of training activity has been undertaken there.

1. Briefings are given to the senior officers and unit commanders. They consist of descriptions of the program and of its practical benefits. The briefings are designed to elicit cooperation and enthusiasm so that these officers will pursue the program aggressively. Spector (1969) realizes that the program will not be effective unless it is supported at high levels.

2. Discussions are held, consisting of 16 one-hour sessions designed for junior officers and enlisted men. Discussion leaders are prepared by additional training. These discussions are often aimed at specific problems and concerns expressed by United States personnel. Spector (1969) wrote of one discussion topic and the method for bringing up significant points:

> For example, many of the men object to the smell of human waste which is used as fertilizer in many developing countries. This practice tends to reinforce the notion that host nationals are inferior. Yet when the men realize that human waste is necessary under present conditions to produce sufficient food to sustain the population, and when they have consciously articulated the preservation of human life as a primary value, they see it as a positive rather than a negative attribute of the host nationals. Their annoyance with the smell is viewed as trivial when measured against the larger need.
>
> The men are encouraged to search for significant reasons for prevailing host national conditions, attitudes, and behavior. They are shown how the struggle for survival—a society's methods for maintaining human life, welfare, and order—is

related to its peoples' feelings of obligation and propriety; how the availability of natural resources affects economic conditions and personal concerns and habits, and so on. The discussions return again and again to first principles and primary factors for elucidation of cross-cultural issues and problems.

Further, the men are encouraged to search their own experiences, the experience of other Americans, or of the U.S. in an earlier day for parallels to the behavior and conditions they find abroad so that they can more readily recognize factors which have contributed to or caused the conditions they meet in the developing world. Thus, it is noted that we too in the United States used human waste extensively before the development of the chemical fertilizer industry, and for precisely the same reason. In this way, the men are provided with conceptual and analytical tools and habits that on the one hand continually reinforce the identity and similarity between themselves and their hosts, and on the other enable them to find the realistic operative reasons for the things and events that they encounter (pp. 16–17).

3. Action programs are, in the writers' opinion, the most important aspect of the training. After the troops have discussed specific problems, as in the previous example, they tend to be less hesitant to engage in action relevant to that problem. At this point in training, they are presented with specific action recommendations. For instance, because a trainee no longer has such negative feelings about human waste used as fertilizer, he may visit a Korean home. The pleasant experiences associated with this action reinforce the positive feelings learned during the discussions. Such actions may be that troops:

a. Learn some of the local language.
b. Spend time with Koreans.
c. Eat Korean meals.
d. Refrain from ridiculing Korean behavior.
e. Avoid derogatory language and names.
f. Encourage peers to take similar actions.

After the first action, such as, eating some Korean food, the soldiers are often interested in learning more. They may ask for information about table manners, what other foods taste like, where to find it, and so forth. It would be useful if the numbers of these behaviors could be documented, because such data is a good measure of program effectiveness.

As training continues, the troops are encouraged to participate in more extensive action programs, for instance:

    a. American soldiers teaching English in Korean schools.

    b. Social gatherings of American soldiers and Korean residents.

    c. Small-Scale community development projects, such as tree planting, farm development, or playground organization.

Evaluation. The evaluation of this program is the most extensive of any within the United States Armed Services, but improvements can still be made. Three evaluative studies have been done in Korea, all of which are summarized in Spector (1969) and Spector et al. (1969).

1. An attitude survey was taken of troops in trained and untrained units. Trained troops reported more favorable attitudes toward host nationals, and felt that Americans (rather than Koreans) had more responsibility for good United States–Korean relations than did untrained troops.

2. In the first step of another evaluation study, ratings were made, both by Army program staff officials and research scientists, concerning which units had effective rather than ineffective programs. Effectiveness was based on the number of lessons presented, the extent to which minimum standards were exceeded, and the like. Soldiers in effective programs reported more favorable attitudes than soldiers in ineffective programs. It is interesting to note that the men in ineffective programs still reported more favorable attitudes than men who were in units that received no training at all.

3. Using the same unit effectiveness ratings, it was shown that Korean soldiers working with Americans in effective units reported better United States–Korean relations than soldiers working with Americans in the ineffective units.

Those researchers who accept attitude measures exclusively as accurate criteria for evaluation will find the above results impressive. Those who feel that attitude measures by themselves are inadequate evaluation criteria, and the writers are among these, will be more critical. We cover such concerns in Chapter four.

Unfortunately, no studies of actual behavior of American troops toward Koreans have been made. Are there fewer fights? Do GIs volunteer free hours to help host nationals? The purpose of training, of course, is to increase incidents of constructive behavior and not to increase the number of favorable verbal or written reports on an attitude scale. This point will be brought out again in the Chapter four, with the caution that there is no established relation between what people say they like and what constructive behavior they will thus engage in.

One problem the program has faced is that although 50,-000 men a year are supposed to receive training, the actual figure is closer to 25,000. Methods must be found to ensure that training takes place within every unit.

The Contrast-American Technique

The Army's Human Resources Research Office (HumRRO) has developed a Contrast-American technique which consists of role-playing encounters between a citizen of the United States and a person of another, simulated culture. Members of this simulated culture hold values in complete contrast to those of Americans; hence the title of the technique. Through interaction with such a person, it is hoped that Americans will develop a self-awareness of their own beliefs, values, and cultural background. This technique is written up in several sources (Stewart, 1966, 1967a, 1967b; Stewart and Pryle, 1966; Danielian, 1967; Danielian and Stewart, 1968; Hoehn, 1968; Kraemer, 1969; Stewart, Danielian, and Foster, 1969).

An overview of the HumRRO work has been given previously in the section (Chapter one) concerning the culture-general versus culture-specific controversy. To review briefly, Kraemer's (1969) summary is quoted. Kraemer presented the belief that improved self-awareness will increase cross-cultural understanding.

. . . training for international assignments might be improved by the inclusion of a process designed to develop the trainee's "cultural self-awareness," that is, his awareness of the cultural nature of *his own* cognitions, particularly of the various subtle ways in which *his own* cultural background will influence him in his interaction with host-country nationals. This means that the trainee would become aware that many of his cognitions, previously thought "natural" or "normal," and therefore universal, may not be shared by members of another culture (p. 2).

This culture-general approach, as Stewart et al. (1969) point out, should be the basis for only one segment, rather than for the entire content of a cross-cultural training program. Other segments would be based on techniques described elsewhere in this book.

Content and trainees. Thirty-five Westinghouse Corporation executives have undergone Contrast-American training under the director of HumRRO personnel. Data gathered from them is reviewed in the next section. In addition, Peace Corps trainees and Army officers at Fort Bragg have participated in role-play encounters.

The American is asked to interact with a person who holds values in contrast to those familiar in the United States. For instance, whereas Americans are optimistic and strive for goals, the Contrast-American is portrayed as fatalistic, believing that his actions have little or no impact on his surroundings.

American values	*Contrast-American values*
Stress material goals	Stress spiritual goals
Achieved status	Ascribed status at birth
Competition viewed as destructive	Competition viewed as constructive
Anticipation of the future	Remembrance of the past
Place reliance on self	Place reliance on superiors and patrons

Role-play situations are then arranged so that some of the values of both the Americans and contrast-culture member will become clear. For example, (Stewart et al., 1969, pp. 30–31):

> One of the scenes was designed around the topic of leadership. During one of the simulations of this scene, Captain Smith, the American role-player, tried to persuade the Contrast-American I, Major Khan, to take measures to improve leadership in his battalion. Captain Smith found fault with some of the techniques utilized by some of Major Khan's second lieutenants.

> American: And I know that . . . if they are allowed to continue, then the efficiency in the duties that they're performing, or their soldiers are performing, will be reduced.

> Contrast-
> American:
> What kind of duties are they performing which are not good?

> A: They have an inability, I think, to communicate with the noncommissioned officers and to properly supervise the accomplishment of the task. They almost have the attitude that this work is the type of work which they should not take part in; they should merely stand by and watch. I know you have a big respect for General George Washington and I should point out this example. One time during the War for Independence, there was a sergeant with some artillery pieces which were stuck. He was standing by, very neat and clean in his uniform, cajoling his soldiers as they looked at him, and shouting for them to push harder to get this cannon out of the mud. General Washington rode by on his horse, noticed this situation and stopped. His rank was not showing, for he had a large cape on over his uniform; it was rather cold that day and had been

raining. He asked the sergeant what the problem was, and the sergeant told him, "Sir, the soldiers cannot get this cannon out of the mud." Then General Washington dismounted from his horse, walked over and assisted the soldiers in pushing the cannon out. Afterward he walked over to the sergeant and said, "Sergeant, tell your commander that General Washington has assisted your men in pushing the cannon from the mud."

CA: Yes.

A: He was willing to assist his men and do anything that they were doing if it were really necessary.

CA: Perhaps if he were not in disguise, not wearing a cape, if he were in his uniform of a general, he would never have come down from (dismounted from) the horse. He would have waited there as a general.

A: I think—

CA: —people would have gotten extra energy while pulling that cannon, they would have looked at him, that big, tall, towering general sitting on a horse, they would have looked at him and derived all inspiration and strength from him, and then pulled out the cannon without his assistance. His very presence would have been enough.

This episode brings out the American desire to get the job done and the Contrast-American's desire to maintain the status relation between the officer and his men. After the encounter, trainees receive feedback about their behavior. Recent efforts have been concerned with the development of videotaped instruction so that many people can receive training by viewing the tapes and no instructors will be needed.

Evaluation. Thirty-five Westinghouse executives completed four tests prior to and 5 days, 9 months, and 21 months after training, making a total of 16 tests for each subject.

Test A measured ability to identify values of Contrast-Americans.

Test B measured ability to predict behavior of Contrast-Americans.

Test C measured knowledge of American predispositions.

Test D measured affective (linking) reactions to American and Contrast-American orientations. The reliability of the tests was determined by pretesting with samples of army officers and Peace Corps trainees.

On Test B (ability to predict Contrast-American behavior), there was a four-point gain from the test taken before training. This gain was maintained 21 months after training. Because the range of the test was 0 to 16, this represents a substantial gain. For test A, there was a gain after training, but it did not hold up as well as Test B after 21 months. Test C gains were minimal. Exact numbers for Test D were not reported, although a statistically insignificant trend (gain) after training was mentioned. Note that the most significant gains (Test B) were in the area of *behavior* prediction rather than attitudes. Roth (1969) feels that training in such behavioral prediction is possible, whereas training to change attitudes may be impossible in the short time alloted for cross-cultural instruction, as pointed out in Chapter one.

Subjective reaction by trainees was reported to be favorable. An interesting note was that the audience reacted more positively when the intercultural aspects of overseas work were studied. In other words, this information on the future of their work assignments may have given the trainees a proper set for learning.

Problems. The HumRRO work has developed without any evidence to support the assumptions underlying the program. For instance, Stewart et al. (1969, p. 4) say:

> While the ultimate desired product of such training is, of course, effective behavior, there is no attempt to teach solutions directly or to provide models for behavior. The purpose is to deal with the cognitive-affective components that underlie behavior, recognizing that increased understanding

and awareness provide the trainee with greater capability and flexibility in meeting the inter-cultural situation effectively.

No rationale is given for not teaching solutions or providing models. These elements may be more important than the elements of the present program.

Kraemer (1969) mentioned that role players complained because they did not have sufficient instructions of a specific nature. This lack may indicate that culture-specific training would be more acceptable to the trainees. It is interesting to note that Stewart recently directed a cross-cultural training program to prepare Catholic nuns for overseas assignment. In an in-house document by Stewart and Rhinesmith (1969), a program for orientation into the Bengali culture was outlined. The training was quite specific, dealing with life, festival, daily chronological, and social events. Perhaps when actual programs are set up (rather than the experimental work reviewed here), the need for specific training becomes clear.

Recent research on the Contrast-American technique has emphasized the use of videotapes, so that large numbers of people might receive training, and the "general" approach of the technique. Kraemer (1973) is critical of most approaches to area training, saying that it is too ethnocentric, focused on a culture's peculiar "foreign-ness," and too abstract in its sociological or anthropological descriptions of that culture. The trainee might become aware of a culture in terms of abstractions and generalities without being able to recognize cultural influences on how people think or behave. The real culture shock may come as we become aware of how much of our own thinking and behavior has been shaped by our own culture, even in ways we would prefer to reject in ourselves and others. The focus of Kraemer's cultural self-awareness approach to cross-cultural orientation is to improve a trainee's ability to recognize cultural influences in his own thinking. This skill would be helpful in identifying problems of intercultural communication in terms of *his own* culture-shaped responses, and not merely in terms of the other person's shortcomings. The nonexpert is otherwise in danger of falsely interpreting a culturally appropriate behavior as a deficiency in the other person's character or intellect.

Greater awareness of our own cultural assumptions should help trainees suspend judgment when confronted by behavior that would otherwise appear odd but which may be a function of how that behavior is *perceived* from our own biased viewpoint. Cultural self-awareness should also contribute to trainees' greater awareness of their ignorance about the other culture, which in turn should motivate them to learn more about that culture. Increased ability to recognize cultural aspects of one's own thinking can result both in more accurate communications and as a stimulus or conceptual tool for learning more about the host culture.

Kraemer (1973) develops his model through the use of videotape recordings of simulated intercultural encounters in which Americans and foreign nationals role played brief encounters. They would then view their own behavior on videotape to identify influences of their own culture and bring about a change in their perception of causes attributed to that behavior. In designing the training program experiences were selected that could have been a trainee's own experience, where cultural influences could be readily identified in spite of other influences, and where the trainees were actively involved in the learning process. Participants were shown staged videotape recordings of an American working overseas and a host national. The actors had a prepared script, but they appeared to be engaging in spontaneous conversations. The excerpts are grouped into sequences, with each sequence showing several different manifestations of a cultural influence focused on a particular issue. The purpose is for participants to view each excerpt and form a tentative hypothesis as to the cultural influence reflected in what the American is saying before they discuss their hypotheses. Their task is to discover the American cultural universals in each sequence with the help of a facilitator.

After some experimentation, the following aspects of American culture were selected for the excerpts: individualism; egalitarianism; action orientation; perception of interpersonal encounters, primarily in terms of their utility, downgrading the social significance of such encounters, the belief that the application of a rule should not be influenced by the relationship between persons applying the rule and those to whom it is applied; definition of persons in terms of their work or achievement; the belief that people to be affected by a decision should have a voice in decision making; the preference for a mode of decision making that evaluates consequences from alternative courses of action; the belief that competition is a good way of motivating people; the belief that there must be differences in "goodness" between various ways of doing something which can be determined and can influence the choice of an alternative; the belief that knowledge through observation is superior to knowledge gained in other ways; unnecessary quantification; placing a higher value on the utility of things than on their aesthetic aspects; problem orientation; the belief that thoughts cannot influence events; reasoning in terms of probability; impatience; the tendency to make comparative judgments; the willingness to offer one's services for the benefit of a common good; the belief in self-help behavior; and the use of absurd suppositions to elicit ideas from other persons.

In research validating this training approach the excerpts were judged quite plausible and believable, even though they were staged. The developers found that it is important for participant's level of cultural self-awareness be somewhat homogeneous; with greater disparity it was difficult to find a level of presentation that would not be too hard for some and too easy for others. Certain minimum levels of intellectual ability and social science education contribute to the design's successful usage, suggesting that some sort of screening of participants might be appropriate. Some participants can be predicted to resist this form of training, especially if they find the exercises unexpectedly difficult or are unable to accept the fact that their own behavior has been culturally influenced. The optimum time for using this exercise was about two days, with another three days to prepare the facilitators, provided that the facilitators already have a good knowledge of intercultural skills and are acquainted with working in small groups.

This model shares many of the assumptions from attribution theory found in the culture assimilator described later in this chapter. In both instances, training should increase a person's ability to select cues from the environment which contribute to interpersonal behavior. To the extent that a person from one culture can successfully predict the behavior of persons from their own culture and the behavior of persons from the other culture *and* in both cases to predict the explanation of that behavior, that person is well prepared to interact in the other culture.

The Self-Confrontation Technique

At Wright-Patterson AFB psychologists conducted a research program in cross-cultural interaction during the mid-1960s. The technique they emphasized was called *self-confrontation*. A trainee role-played with another person in a simulated cross-cultural encounter, the entire episode being videotaped. After the role-playing, the trainee and trainer played back the tape, criticizing weak points in both verbal and nonverbal behavior. Trainees then role-played the same or a similar situation again so that learning could be measured. The technique has been written up in many documents, which we will summarize and review. (Haines, 1964; Haines and Eachus, 1965; Eachus, 1965, 1966a, 1966b; Eachus and King, 1966; King, 1966, 1967a, 1967b; Gael, 1967).

Experimental method and evaluation. Three experiments were conducted. Study 1 used college undergraduates as subjects, study 2 used military volunteers, and study 3 used officers (first lieutenants through lieutenant colonels) from a Psychological Operations and Civic Action (POCA) course. The first two studies compared a self-confrontation group of trainees against a control group who read descriptions of the other culture. The third study did not have a control group, but it did compare the performance of the officers to subjects from studies 1 and 2.

In the first two studies, self-confrontation subjects read introductory material about a fictitious country X and a description of the roleplay situation suggesting specific verbal and nonverbal behaviors that would lead to effective interaction. The following passage is an example of this material (Eachus and King, 1966, p. 4).

> You will play the part of Captain Brown, the head of a United States Air Force Mobile Training unit. The team is to train certain components of the Country "X" Air Force in the latest air-drop and night flying operations . . . You are in an extremely important position requiring not only technical skill, but also interpersonal skill in dealing with personnel in the Air Force of Country "X" . . . the failure of the Americans to observe or respect traditional Country "X" customs and protocol usually is misunderstood and misinterpreted. Such circumstances could seriously affect the success of the training mission.

The experimental subjects then role-played, had their videotape criticized, then role-played again. Control subjects were given reading material for the same amount of time that role-play subjects spent being taped and criticized. Control subjects then role-played so that a comparison could be made between their performance and the experimental subjects.

In the second role-play situation, self-confrontation (experimental) subjects performed better in verbal and nonverbal behaviors than did the subjects who had spent the early part of the experiment reading. The experimenters interpreted this as showing the value of the self-confrontation technique. In addition, the self-confrontation subjects retained more than 90 percent of their learning measured at the end of a 2-week interval.

In the third study, the Air Force officers did not study country *X*. Rather, they studied Iran. Their interaction with an actor simulating an Iranian was videotaped and then replayed so that criticisms could be made. The officers showed an increase in learning from the first to the second role-play encounter. They performed better on both these occasions than the subjects in studies 1 and 2. The experimenters interpreted this finding as showing that the officers were more highly motivated and were representative of a more select population. No retention data was gathered. The experimenters had hoped to measure behavior during actual overseas assignment of these and/or similar officers, but funds for the project were discontinued.

Problems. Although the Air Force researchers claimed highly favorable results for the self-confrontation technique, we need to consider several alternative explanations. We do not mean to be overly critical; rather, we are trying to point out the type of analysis that should be done before making claims about a technique.

1. Self-confrontation subjects might have done better than control subjects in the second role-playing encounter simply because they were more familiar and comfortable with the videotape equipment. Rather than any cultural learning during the first encounter and subsequent criticism, self-confrontation subjects may have been more self-assured and comfortable in front of the television camera than the control subjects. The control subjects, after all, were taped only once, the experimental subjects twice. Colleagues who work with complex machines and instruments agree with this analysis. In general, people often do poorly with unfamiliar equipment that *should* aid them because the people are simply uncomfortable with the equipment.

2. The officer subjects in study 3 interacted with a person from an actual country, Iran, rather than country X. They may have performed better than earlier subjects not because they were from a more select population but because they were interested in studying a real country. This criticism is similar to the one made of the HumRRO contrast-culture technique. We feel that using material about a real country will arouse more interest and encourage more real learning than using materials about simulated cultures.

3. The retention data taken only 2 weeks after the first training session is not too impressive. In actual assignment, people must interact with foreign nationals months and years after training.

4. The cost of the technique may be prohibitive for use in training large numbers of people because every person undergoing training must engage in an interaction that is video-

taped, and then a trainer has to review the videotape. Video-tape is expensive (as is the equipment to record the interactions), and the review can be very time consuming. Hence the technique may be impractical for widespread use.

The self-confrontation technique needs more evaluation to show if it is indeed useful for cross-cultural training. We do not want to be more harsh on this technique than others. As is pointed out in Chapter four, few cross-cultural training techniques have been subjected to enough empirical investigation to inspire absolute confidence. The developers of the self-confrontation technique deserve credit for presenting their work in clear, precise write-ups so that outside reviewers can comment on their work.

Shore Leave Exchanges

Since May of 1961, the United States Navy has sponsored an overseas orientation program under the direction of David Rosenberg. The training consists of a 3-hour demonstration and subsequent discussions. The specific purpose is to prepare Americans for pleasant and trouble-free liberty in foreign ports. The emphasis of the training is on the person-to-person relations between Americans and host nationals. Information about the program was gathered from articles by Smith (1961), Clarke (1963), Mapes (1967), David (1968), and a short summary by program director, David Rosenberg (1970) as well as several discussions with him.

The vast majority of trainees have been sailors about to go on liberty in foreign ports. Well over 750,000 men have gone through the program. Through the request of others, however, the program has been given to dependants of active-duty personnel, reserve units, Army personnel at Ft. Bragg, congressmen, the State Department, educational institutions (including the U.S. Naval Academy), and foreign nationals.

Rosenberg organizes and carries out the orientations as an employee of the Department of the Navy on a full-time basis. The program is a one-man show, with Rosenberg travelling to all Navy ports around the world. It is difficult to convey the spirit of the 3-hour demonstration. Rosenberg is a folk-dancer (expert), linguist, stand-up comic, magician, tour guide, slide-show commentator, and "old-salt." He possesses a tremendous amount of information about most countries, and always has books to find answers to questions that come up during discussion periods. Most of the time the books are not needed. The atmosphere is that of a three-ring circus with Rosenberg prancing about, performing dance steps, putting on different costumes, throwing candy, and giving very practical advice on how to have a good time and stay out of trouble. He brings along many flags, road signs, and large souvenirs to show his audience. He covers drinking (but begs his audience not to get drunk), meeting host nationals, getting dates, buying worthwhile souvenirs, and respecting local customs. Mapes (1967) wrote:

> American servicemen, of course, are constantly barraged with films, booklets, chaplains' talks and medical lectures urging them to stay out of trouble in foreign lands. But the Navy's over-seasmanship program is unique in that it speaks to sailors in their own language. The service hopes that with a little of Dave's entertaining prodding, sailors will forsake the time-honored dockside gin mills to see something of the countries they visit and spread some American goodwill in the process.

Rosenberg exploits the talents and interests of the members of his audience. Before he arrives on board, sailors fill out a "skill finder," a questionnaire asking each person what his interests are, what dances can he do, what instruments can he play, what skills can he teach others, and the like. After the answers are summarized by personnel on the ship, Rosenberg knows how to best address his audience. He brings strangers together who have the same skills and points out where these groups can pursue their interests in the host country. A major point of emphasis is that Americans should know the diversity of customs and practices in their own country so that experiences in foreign countries will not be so strange. In face-to-face interactions after the demonstration, he draws individuals out, chatting about mutual interests, giving as much information as he can. He tells the sailors "what's in it for them." He encourages sailors to try new experiences rather than sit in bars and tourist traps that cater to Americans. Rosenberg realizes that Americans would like to have pleasant liberty, doing new things, if they only knew how. The purpose of the program is to give such instruction, showing the trainee how to be comfortable in another culture. Information is specific (e.g., in Spain, don't cheer the bull at bullfights; in Oslo, don't hail a cab, call one. If Rosenberg were to prepare crews about to leave for a tour in Latin America, specific information about those countries would be presented).

Data on program effectiveness is minimal and anecdotal. Navy officials are convinced that the program has decreased the number of sailors who were arrested or made trouble during liberty. For instance, Rosenberg presented his program to several ships before a recent cruise to South America, and it is reported that there were no arrests in 23,000 individual liberties. Many unsolicited letters have been received by officers and enlisted men explaining that they found the program valuable. Rosenberg's program has been part of three major network television programs and a *Wall Street Journal* article. There have, however, been no formal evaluative studies of the program. Having met David Rosenberg and seen his demonstration, it is difficult not to be enthusiastic about the program. Evaluation studies, however, will be useful in pointing out aspects that could be expanded or discarded.

The Culture Assimilator

Social scientists at the University of Illinois have developed and evaluated the Culture Assimilator, a training technique that has been subjected to more empirical study than any other. The information presented here was gathered from several summary statements of the research (Triandis, 1968, 1975; Fiedler, 1969; Fiedler, Mitchell and Triandis, 1971) and the work of Foa and Chemers (Foa and Chemers, 1967; Mitchell and Foa, 1968; Chemers, 1968).

The goal of assimilator training is to prepare trainees for

specific interpersonal situations in a specific country. In addition, training should "expose members of one culture to some of the basic concepts, attitudes, role perceptions, customs and values of another culture" (Fiedler et al., 1971, p. 95). Since training is culture-specific, there is a different assimilator for every pair of cultures. That is, assimilators are designed so that members of one given culture (e.g., the United States) learn about another (e.g., Iran).

The culture assimilator is comprised of a series of episodes that previous visitors to a given country have labeled as problem situations. Each episode describes an interaction between a visitor (Americans, in the examples below) and a host national. After reading about the interactions, trainees examines four different interpretations. If trainees make the right choice that best explains the interaction, they are reinforced. If they make a mistake, they are told why their choice is wrong and are asked to restudy the episode and make another choice. Trainees proceed at their own rate, and no trainee can proceed beyond any one incident until he or she has discovered the correct interpretation of that interaction between people.

Assimilators have been developed for the Arab countries, Thailand, Iran, Greece, India, and Honduras (all available in technical reports from the University of Illinois). An assimilator for black-white relations within the United States has recently been developed. The interaction incidents are validated by asking host nationals to give the correct answer, without seeing any of the alternatives. The host nationals also indicate how important the story is and how frequently they feel it might occur. All incidents must score high on these ratings. After these indices of agreement, importance, and probable occurrence are used to discard nonuseful incidents, the assimilator contains 75 to 100 episodes, from an original pool of 150 to 200.

The example below is from the Thai assimilator. The incident:

Page X-1

One day a Thai administrator of middle academic rank kept two of his assistants waiting about an hour from an appointment. The assistants, although very angry, did not show it while they waited. When the administrator walked in at last, he acted as if he were not late. He made no apology or explanation. After he was settled in his office, he called his assistants in and they all began working on the business for which the administrator had set the meeting.

The four alternatives, one of which explains the incident, are then presented:

If you had happened to observe the incident exactly as it is reported in this passage, which one of the following would you say describes the chief significance of the behavior of the people involved?

1. The Thai assistants were extremely skillful at concealing their true feelings.

Go to Page X-3

2. The Thai administrator obviously was unaware of the fact that he was an hour late for the appointment.

Go to Page X-4

3. In Thailand, subordinates are required to be polite to their superiors, no matter what happens, nor what their rank may be.

Go to Page X-5

4. Clearly, since no one commented on it, the behavior indicated nothing of any unusual significance to any of the Thais.

Go to Page X-6

Trainees then turn to the page indicated by the alternative they chose.

Page X-3

You selected 1: The Thai assistants were extremely skillfull at concealing their true feelings.

This is not entirely correct.

It is quite characteristic of Thais to try to appear reserved under any circumstances. If the assistants were extremely skillful at concealing their true feelings, would you know that you weren't seeing their true feelings? Also, does the reference to the chief significance of the behavior of "the people involved" limit it to the assistant?

Go to Page X-1

Page X-4

You selected 2: The Thai administrator obviously was unaware of the fact that he was an hour late for the appointment.

A very poor choice.

While the administrator acted as if he were unaware of his tardiness after observing the hour's wait, don't you suspect that perhaps he was acting?

Go to Page X-1

Page X-5

You selected 3: In Thailand, subordinates are required to be polite to their superiors, no matter what happens, nor what their rank may be.

Very good. You are utilizing the information in the episodes to its fullest extent. Continue. This is the correct response.

To some extent their "deference to the boss" may be observed almost anywhere in the world, but you are far more likely to find it carried to a higher degree in Thailand than in the United States.

There were certain clues to help you select 3: the assistants' concealed feelings, the administrator's failure to apologize, the fact that no one mentioned the tardiness, and the subsequent keeping of the appointment which the administrator had set.

Did you use them all?

What you've already learned from earlier sections of the culture assimilator can help you. What did you learn about respect for older and higher status persons in Thailand? And about the attitude of students toward an American professor?

Go to Page Y-1

[the next incident]

You selected 4: Clearly, since no one commented on it, the behavior indicated nothing of any unusual significance to any of the Thais.

This is completely wrong.

While the behavior reported in the passage does not seem so significant for the Thais in this relationship as it might be to Americans, why was nothing said about the tardiness? And why were the assistants "very angry" although they "did not show it?"

Isn't there a more significant level of meaning for this behavior?

Go to Page X-1

Foa and Chemers (1967) suggested that success in cross-cultural interaction may be dependent on knowledge of the differentiation of roles in different countries. For instance, in some countries residents do not distinguish the role of woman and the role of high-status leader; that is, women can never be leaders in some countries (the roles are not differentiated). In certain countries (e.g., the United States), people can have a heated argument in the role of work partners and then go happily off to a social engagement together. This role differentiation does not occur in the Middle East. Foa and Chemers (1967, pp. 50–51) presented the following incident and an analysis.

Haluk, an Arab exchange student, was working on a class project with several American students. At a meeting of the project staff, the Arab student was asked to give his suggestions concerning the way the project should be carried out. Immediately after he finished talking, Jim, one of the American associates, raised his hand and said in a clear voice that he disagreed with Haluk's proposals. Then he pointed out a number of specific difficulties that Haluk's approach would incur for the project as a whole and its staff. After the meeting, Haluk told Jim and another student on the project that he would not be able to go to the movies with them as they had planned because he had just remembered he had to get a book out of the library to prepare for a class the next day. When the two boys expressed disappointment and suggested that they could go the next evening, Haluk politely told them that he had already had another appointment for the next evening.

Assume that you were the other student who had planned to go to the movies with Jim and Haluk after the meeting. Which of the following thoughts would you regard as most likely to be a correct analysis of the situation as you went off to the movies with Jim?

A. Haluk was certainly a more serious student than you and Jim. Go to page. . . .

B. Haluk was offended because Jim had disagreed with his ideas in front of others. Go to page. . . .

C. Jim really should have been listened more carefully while Haluk was talking. Go to page. . . .

D. Jim always talked loud, but this shouting in the meeting had been unnecessary. Go to page. . . .

E. You should have gone to the library with Haluk. Go to page. . . .

The hypothesis proposes that the differentiation between systems, in terms of status and affect, will be less strong in the Middle Eastern than in the American culture. In this story, Haluk is denied status by Jim in the work system. Haluk transfers this denial to the leisure system, in terms of affect, i.e., Haluk feels: "If Jim denies me status at work, this means he also denies me affect, so I must not give affect (go to the movies) to him." The correct explanation for the Middle Eastern culture, as suggested both by the assimilator and the hypothesis is B. The American, Jim, differentiates more than his Arab friend between work and leisure, so for him the relationship between denial of status in work and denial of affect in leisure is not as strong as for Haluk.

Evaluation. Studies reviewed by Fiedler et al. (1971), and Nayar, Touzard, and Summers (1968) support the usefulness of assimilator training. Two laboratory studies using Arab and Thai assimilators compared American subjects who had received training with other subjects who had received instruction in geography. The geography subjects were a control group for measuring the effects of attention, that is, attention from prestigious people (in this case, the researchers), no matter what the content of the training. Both studies showed that assimilator training lessened interpersonal and adjustment problems in actual contact between Americans and foreign nationals. However, group productivity was not increased as a function of assimilator versus geography training.

The one field study that has been conducted compared teenage volunteer workers in Honduras who had received assimilator training with those who had not. An independent performance measure, made by the program director and his staff members (who had no "investment" in the culture assimilator), was the major criterion or dependent variable. Adjustment measures were also gathered from the teenagers themselves. Results showed that the assimilator-trained groups were superior on both measures to the groups who had not received assimilator training. An unexpected finding was that teenagers who had participated in the project the previous year had better performance ratings than first-year volunteers. This finding may indicate that assimilator training helps people who have already spent time in a foreign country to integrate their previous cultural experiences.

Problems. 1. Not enough field assessment has been done, as the developers have pointed out.

2. The best content for assimilators has not been determined. Should they contain information about interpersonal attitudes, customs, value contrasts, and so on, or some mix? Triandis (1975) has suggested that many of the incidents can be written about people's misattributions concerning the behavior of others. That is, a person from culture A may see someone from culture B behave in a certain way, and might diagnose incorrectly the reasons for the behavior. The story of the Arab student, Haluk, who mistakenly attributed Jim's be-

havior to hostile feelings is an example. Triandis (1975) calls for incidents that will increase "isomorphic attribution," or the same diagnosis of the behavior on the part of all people in a given cross-cultural interaction.

3. If similarities between the cultures are to be emphasized, there are few data to show what types of topics should bring out the similarities. Furthermore, it is difficult to determine when similarities or differences between cultures should be emphasized.

4. Evaluation to date has been conducted using subjects of high motivation and/or intelligence. These people may not be typical of all people who might receive training.

Future Goals. Triandis (1968) indicated the following goals for future assimilator training:

1. Make the assimilator more flexible to the individual trainee's needs.

2. Present information so as not to arouse defensiveness and hostility.

3. Emphasize the most attractive aspects of the foreign culture.

4. Provide the trainee with skills in effective interaction, flexibility in response to different situations, ability to suspend judgment, and appreciation of cultural differences.

The culture assimilator is a valuable tool and can easily become a part of training programs. The incidents take time to develop, but, once established, are very useful and can be incorporated into a variety of cross-cultural programs, as discussed throughout this book. Our lengthy treatment of problems is again due to the developers' willingness to be very open about their technique, and this encourages input from others. As a personal note, we have found the culture-assimilator approach useful in our own work. We have often combined the written assimilator incidents with group discussion, because the incidents quickly stimulate comment from people who have read them, and people become anxious to share their reactions with others.

The Peace Corps Program

The Peace Corps has been established to prepare and then send Americans to various countries for different types of social action (e.g., teaching, construction, farming, health-related) projects. Several studies have been conducted on the Peace Corps training program to prepare people for different countries, most of it from the "earlier days" of the organization (about 1960 to 1966). Recently, as Harris (1973) points out, there has not been as much research, and certainly not the number of extremely competent social scientists working for the Peace Corps as there were in those earlier days. Several of the findings from this body of research are directly relevant to the purposes of this book.

Research findings. Prior to about 1970, at the end of training and before deployment overseas, administrators of Peace Corps programs evaluated the potential success of volunteers. Several independent investigators (Guthrie and Zektick, 1967; Stein, 1963; Smith, Fawcett, Ezekiel, and Roth, 1963) have shown that evaluations at end of training do not correlate (have no relation) to evaluation of performance in the field. In the Guthrie and Zektick, (1967) study, Peace Corps volunteers on assignment in the Philippines were evaluated there by both American officials and host nationals. Neither rating of effectiveness correlated with the volunteers' success measured after training back in the United States. Guthrie (1969, 1975) explains these findings by pointing out that the expectations about behavior and ways to obtain rewards in the United States are well known to its residents. After assignment to another culture, however, expectations and rewards are much less clear. It seems that a person effective in the United States is not necessarily effective in the different environment of the foreign culture. Many people have heard stories about missionaries who were rated average, ineffective, or downright incompetent by a big-city church in the United States but who were very comfortable and productive in primitive villages overseas. These missionaries were able to meet the expectations of the village (e.g., personal contact, sincerity) but not the big city (e.g., skill at fund raising, ability to lecture to large groups).

The important point to be remembered is that assessment of knowledge or predicted effectiveness after training in the United States is not sufficient. Assessment must be carried out in the host country if at all possible.

Another series of studies documented the advantage of "follow-on" training. Arnold (1967) established a program to provide training during assignment in the host culture. Noting that American volunteers had adjustment problems, especially during the first 6 months, Arnold started discussion groups, called *follow-on training*, because it was done after the volunteers' assignment. All Peace Corps members in a certain area were brought together frequently to discuss any issue that they desired. Adjustment and culture shock problems were often brought up. In addition, the meetings provided social support for the members. Arnold noted that the number of the premature returns (volunteers who go back to the United States before 2-year assignment is up) for the discussion group members was only 25 percent of the figure for nonparticipating volunteers in similar cultures. The comparison data were from Thomson and English (1963; 1964). This criterion is not perfect, of course, but it does provide a behavioral measure that is more valuable than asking the discussion group members how much they like their assignment.

The important point to be remembered from this Peace Corps experience is that training before assignment should be complemented by additional training at different points during residence in the foreign culture.

Several researchers (Thomson and English, 1963; Dobyns, Doughty, and Holmberg, 1965) have investigated the satisfaction and effectiveness of volunteers during their assignment. Their findings indicate:

1. Volunteers who are able to use their skills (e.g., teacher, farmer) are more satisfied than volunteers who are assigned to a job in which their skills are not needed. The premature return rate was lower for those using their skills.

2. Volunteers who are skillful in the language of the host culture, and/or who interact frequently with host nationals are

more effective as measured by the number of projects implemented.

These points indicate that cross-cultural training should complement skill training (a point also made by R. Campbell, 1969) since people may be unhappy if their skills aren't used in the host country. The findings also indicate that training should emphasize language skills and encourage interaction with host nationals.

Kerrick, Clark, and Rice (1967) and Haigh (1966) investigated certain cross-cultural training techniques. Haigh suggested that trainees spend time in an American subculture (e.g., a ghetto area or an Appalachian mountain community) prior to overseas assignment. Haigh's group of volunteers worked on an American Indian reservation as part of their training. This is similar to the recommendation (Guthrie, 1963; Bennington College, 1958) that a foreign national be a part of the training team. Unfortunately, the only evaluation of Haigh's (1966) suggestion is the enthusiastic response by the trainees.

Kerrick et al. (1967) found that a lecture was more effective than a discussion group in persuading Peace Corps volunteers to adopt certain health practices. This apparently contradicts the often-cited finding from Lewin's (1947) and Coch and French's (1948) work that group discussion is superior to a lecture in persuading housewives to change eating habits and persuading factory workers to adopt a new production method. The reconciliation comes when it is explained that volunteers didn't have much to say about health practices because they were still learning about them. The subjects in the Lewin and Coch–French studies knew their material and could discuss it. The important point is that group discussion will be effective only when the trainees know enough about the topic to discuss it.

The University-Alternative Model. The article by Harrison and Hopkins (1967), presenting a cross-cultural training model, contrasts university education with the type of education necessary for overseas work. The greatest weakness is that university learning does not deal with interpersonal relations, that is, the human rather than technical aspects of overseas work. The goals of university and cross-cultural education and methods of learning are presented side-by-side to emphasize the need for new training techniques. Some examples:

University Education

Communication: To communicate fluently via the written word and, to a lesser extent, to speak well is one goal, as is the ability to master the languages of abstraction and generalization, such as mathematics and science. To understand readily the reasoning, the ideas, and the knowledge of other persons through verbal exchange is another goal.

Problem Solving: A problem is solved when the true, correct, reasonable answer has been discovered and verified. Problem solving is a search for knowledge and truth. It is a largely rational process, involving intelligence, creativity, insight, and a respect for facts.

Source of Information: Information comes from experts and authoritative sources through the media of books, lectures, audio-visual presentations. "If you have a question, look it up."

Role of Emotions and Values: Problems are largely dealt with at an ideational level. Questions of reason and of fact are paramount. Feelings and values may be discussed but are rarely acted upon.

Overseas Education

Communications: To understand and communicate directly and often nonverbally through movement, facial expression, person-to-person actions is one goal, as is the ability to listen with sensitivity to the hidden concerns, values, motives of the other. To be at home in the exchange of feelings, attitudes, desires, fears, and to have a sympathetic, *empathic* understanding of the feelings of the other are other goals.

Problem Solving: A problem is solved when decisions are made and carried out that effectively apply people's energies to overcoming some barrier to a common goal. Problem solving is a social process involving communication, interpersonal influence, consensus, and commitment.

Source of Information: Information sources must be developed by the learner from the social environment. Information-gathering methods include observation and questioning of associates, other learners, and chance acquaintances.

Role of Emotions and Values: Problems are usually value- and emotion-laden. Facts are often less relevant than the perceptions and attitudes people hold. Values and feelings have action consequences, and action must be taken.

Harrison and Hopkins then list the goals of their proposed program. Trainees should:

1. Develop the ability to become more independent of external sources of information and problem definition.

2. Develop the ability to deal with feelings created by value conflicts.

3. Be able to make decision in stressful situations.

4. Be able to use own and others' feelings as information.

A training program was then established for 82 Peace Corps volunteers being assigned to Ecuador, Chile, and Bolivia. The 10-week training program had these characteristics:

1. From their arrival, the trainees were encouraged to participate actively in the planning of their program. In a sense, there would be no program unless *they* planned it by determining what kind of training program was needed in order to reach the objectives *they* had formulated.

2. Formal classroom lectures were played down; small-group interaction was played up, as was informal interaction of all kinds.

3. Except for Spanish (4 hours a day) and weekly evaluation sessions (to be discussed later), attendance at the "happenings" of the program was *not* be compulsory.

4. An effort was made to do away with component labels and thus to "integrate" the elements of the program.

5. The program was experience based. There were ample opportunities furnished for doing things, such as organizing and operating coops, raising chickens and pigs, planting and tending gardens, and approaching academic subjects through research projects. Trainees with needed skills were urged to teach them to others, formally or informally. The emphasis, in short, was on trainee activity, not passivity.

6. Emphasis was placed throughout on awareness of the environment of the training program and of what was going on and how the trainees were reacting to it (and to one an-

other). This was to be achieved through weekly small-group evaluation sessions. The personnel of these core groups, including the leaders, would remain fairly constant throughout the program.

It is interesting to us that some of the elements of the alternative approach have been accepted by American universities involved in nontraditional approaches to education. Unfortunately, no data were gathered on program effectiveness; in fact, the writers made a point of saying that no data-collection efforts were made. We feel that it is valuable to present a summary of the program; however, because the Harrison–Hopkins model has sound ideas that should be subjected to empirical research. Our analysis is that the lack of data in the cross-cultural training literature as a whole forces people to accept the nonempirical but provocative Harrison–Hopkins article (it has been reprinted frequently). This problem is discussed further in Chapter four.

The area simulation model. The simulation of a village or household from some foreign country was one technique used by the Peace Corps in training. The basic idea was to duplicate a model of the foreign country as a training laboratory. When the area simulation site shared inherent similarities with the target environment, such as Puerto Rico for training Peace Corps volunteers for Latin America, the Virgin Islands for volunteers for West Africa, or Hawaii for Southeast Asian volunteers, the area simulation model seemed an attractive training approach. As Downs (1969) points out, the basic, fundamental differences between a training situation and the field situation were too often glossed over, leaving trainees with a superficial and oversimplified characterization of reality which may have done more to distort their perception of the host culture than to help them make an eventual adjustment.

Importing water buffalos and building Southeast Asian villages in the Waipio Valley of Hawaii, besides being very expensive, was never able to prove its success as a training model. There was a "Disneyland" attractiveness to the model which has proven its commercial value in projects such as the Polynesian Village in Hawaii or Williamsburg, Virginia, to mention several locations where tourists have no doubt gained some insights into another culture by participating in a simulated community from that culture. To the extent that the simulation is authentic, the training is certainly valuable. Some aspects of area simulation can probably be incorporated usefully into other programs of cross-cultural orientation. However, by itself, this approach has not been a successful approach to in-depth training for cross-cultural orientation. In-country training programs have virtually replaced the area simulation model as an environment-oriented training approach for the Peace Corps. In-country programs have incorporated many of its advantages while eliminating much of the expense and many of the superficial objections to this model.

Reorientation Seminars at the East-West Center

The East-West Center is an international educational institution situated on the main campus of the University of Hawaii. Over 1000 participants each year come from the United States and 40 countries and territories in Asia and the Pacific area. There are three types of participants (degree students, professional development students, and fellows), but we are most concerned with degree students in this presentation. These participants almost always have the equivalent of a Bachelor's degree from a school in their home countries, and they come to the East-West Center both to participate in its programs and to earn Master's (sometimes Ph.D.) degrees at the University of Hawaii. The participants, then, are away from their homes for an average of 2 years while studying at the East-West Center. There are certainly numerous advantages to the rich experience of living and working with the many types of people one meets at the center, but it is not all a bed of Plumeria petals.

When people live in a culture other than their own for a significant length of time, their attitudes and outlook change (Bochner, 1973a; Useem and Useem, 1955, 1968; Cleveland et al., 1960). Many aspects of the home country will also have changed, for instance, the attitudes of their friends and family and the physical elements of the environment that they remember. An interesting and important fact which has emerged from research in recent years (Bochner, 1973b) is that a person who is most successful at adjusting to a new culture is often the worst at readjusting to the old culture. Perhaps the explanation is that a person who adjusts readily is one who can accept new ideas, meet and talk intelligently with people from many countries, and be happy with the stimulation that he or she finds every day. This same person may readjust poorly upon returning home, since the new ideas conflict with tradition. The returnee finds no internationally minded people, and can find no stimulation in the country he or she already knows so well. Training to prepare people for such reverse culture shock problems has been uncommon. For these reasons, the first author of this book has been involved in research on reorientation cross-cultural seminars, sometimes called the "Can you go home again?" program.[2] Since there are so few *re*orientation programs, we review it in more detail than other cross-cultural programs.

The seminars involve East-West Center grantees who are about to return home after a 2-year stay in Hawaii. The seminars include participants from the United States, because few of them will return to hometowns in which they will have daily contact with friends from Asia and the Pacific. Actually, the readjustment to home can be most severe for participants from the United States, because they do not expect any problems. Instead, they maintain that "I'm not going back to another country!" It is argued that in many ways they *are* going from one culture (the State of Hawaii and the East-West Center) to another (somewhere on the mainland).

Basis of the approach within the seminar. The theoretical basis for the seminar is that of Janis (1958; see also the summary presentation by Elms, 1972) who wrote about preparation for stressful events. Using the concept, "the work of worrying," he argued that if a person worries about potentially stressful events, this worrying activity is helpful. Such work can force the person to learn as much as possible about the event, to prepare for its negative effects so as not to be surprised by them, and to envisage what she might do if any of the negative

[2]Work on the program has been done in conjunction with H. Van Buren (Brislin and Van Buren, 1974).

effects indeed occur. The principle has widespread application, and Janis has made one specific recommendation for its use with surgical patients. Here, the principle suggest that patients should be told basic facts about their upcoming operations and should work through in their minds exactly how they might feel. This practice would be in contrast to the more common procedure in which patients are told little or nothing about how they will feel after an operation. The goal is to have people not be taken by surprise when they feel the inevitable postoperational pain. Instead, they should have worked the pain through in their minds prior to the surgery and consequently be less effected by it.

In an impressive study by Egbert et al. (1964), the recommendations were put to use in a hospital. After their operations, the worry-prepared patients felt less emotional stress, were given less pain-killing medication, and were released from the hospital an average of 3 days sooner than control patients who did not undergo such preparation. The release recommendations, incidentally, were given by doctors who did not know which group a given patient was in, worry-prepared or control.

Based on this work, East-West Center grantees are asked, just before they return home, to work out potential difficulties in their minds. Participants are not told that they *will have* such problems, but rather that the possibility exists. We reiterate this point because it has been the basis of confrontation from some staff members at the East-West Center. The charge has been made that people are told what will happen, and that this is paternalistic. The response is simple: this is not true.

Content of the East-West Center reorientation. Each of several session is begun by a kickoff speaker who brings up different issues that should stimulate thinking, then participants have an open discussion. Kickoff speakers always present specific difficulties *they* and others have faced, and we include these here because they give an idea of both a session's content and the issues brought up in free discussion. The participants do almost all the talking for 75 to 80 percent of any given session, the kickoff speaker and other staff members giving input for the remaining time.

A. FAMILY AND PERSONAL ASPECTS OF RETURNING HOME.

Emphasis is on relations with one's mother, father, siblings, and friends. At every seminar, at least one person was about to return home (Asia) and be faced with an arranged marriage, and these people had been dating freely in Hawaii. At a recent seminar, the kickoff speaker was an American who told about his own stress in returning from Japan to Akron, Ohio. If speakers relate their own experiences (as they have done at every seminar), it helps greatly; it becomes clear to participants that the readjustment is a normal process and that they are not kooks if they are faced with a problem.

The following is from a former participant's letter, and it is typical of the examples given by the speakers.

> One of the most difficult things to adjust to was living at home with my family. Being single and working in the same city as my home, it is generally expected that the student stay with his family. The warmth and security at home was one of the things I missed most while abroad. It was lacking for the 2–3 years I was away and the forced independence being away from home became something I grew accustomed to; living in a dorm or apartment, not having to tell my whereabouts all the time, washing and cooking, traveling alone. Things such as these which were considered of positive survival value (independence) is not acceptable at one's own home. Even among friends, I felt there was more need to conform. Disagreement or refusal to anyone at home or my friends was regarded as rejection of them as friends more so than in the USA where it was taken as differences of opinion or just being in the mood for something else. There is little opportunity to be *alone* at home, nor is it regarded as good. It was hard to change from home-living to apartment-living abroad, but it is perhaps even harder to change back again.

B. SHORT TERM AND LONG TERM ADJUSTMENTS

The emphasis here is on the issues that would be problematic over a short period of time. The recommendation is that a person should not be overwhelmed by short-term problems and should not feel that "I'm making a poor readjustment" if small problems are immediately troublesome. For instance, adjusting to the custom concerning which sex walks through doors first is a short-term problem, whereas advancing on the job is a long-term issue. Another recommendation is for participants who want to change their old culture. Advice is given concerning change of smaller, more manageable aspects rather than the culture as a whole. From a letter:

> Now that I am back, I realize how difficult it will be for me to use my East-West Center studies to change the curriculum in my department. I want to put the "new math" into my school and follow it through all four grades and see how it works. I am enthusiastic about this new way of teaching math.
>
> But before I can even plan any new curriculum, I must convince my principal and the staff of the school that this is a worthwhile change. There is strong resistance, especially from older teachers. They have been here a long time, and do not have any modern training in how to teach mathematics. Just a suggestion of change makes them uneasy and resistant.
>
> I believe it may take me two years before I can convince the staff to let me try my new ideas. But I think it is very important that I not give up, but keep trying. I am now thinking of how this can be done. . . ."

C. RETURN TO JOBS AND COLLEAGUES

This session is similar to A, the difference being that the speakers, and subsequent participant discussion, center around professional relations on the job rather than relations with family members. Especially vivid examples have been given by speakers. A staff member from Japan has reported that Japanese often *hide* the fact that they have an American college degree, because it is not as useful in job advancement as an in-country degree. A staff member from the Philippines emphasized how she is especially careful about interpersonal relations there, since such relations are much more sensitive and can interfere with work to a greater degree than in the United States. The following is a letter that was written by a person whose *colleague* had received an East-West Center grant. Incidentally, this is the first author's favorite discussion starter.

Dear Mr. ——

Please pardon me for writing suddenly to you to ask a favor of you. My name is. . . . I am a teacher of English at Senior High School in Kyoto, Japan. I am 39 years old, so I'm not qualified to the admission to your university. However I want to study English at your university by all means. Is it quite impossible for you to lift the age limit from 35 to about 45? I very much want you to make your utmost efforts to lift the limit. I sincerely hope you will give me an opportunity, a fair opportunity to receive education at your university. You might think that it's troublesome to teach a 40-year-old student, but I hope you'll teach a student who is very eager to study, though he may be rather old.

To tell the truth, one of my fellow teachers is going to enter your university. He and I live in the same small town, and I am his superior at our school. In this situation, it is impossible for me to continue staying at the present school, he will be greatly respected as an English teacher by all the teachers and students at our school and the inhabitants of our small town. On the other hand it is easy to guess what will happen to me. They will come to think nothing of me, to be sure. I have been worried for the past several months.

I sincerely hope you'd try to lift the age limit again.

Sincerely yours,

D. ROLE PLAYING AND VIDEO TAPING

Participants were asked to prepare short skits, acting out what might happen after they return home. Participants were given the option of writing a script or simply writing down a few ideas which they would develop as the role play or skits continued. The skits were videotaped and played back to the staff and participants immediately on a television monitor. Videotaping increases the impact (Bailey and Sowder, 1970; also the section in this chapter on the self-confrontation technique), and adds to the popularity of the session, for everyone enjoys seeing himself on television. Over the three seminars, almost all the participants have chosen to be somewhat humorous in their skits, reinforcing our recommendation made in other sessions to keep a light heart concerning readjustment.

Obviously, all roles such as father, mother, and boss are played by participants. Some of the skits went as follows:

1. A returning son shows slides of the East-West Center to his parents, and they comment on the scanty clothing of the girls and also talk about an arranged marriage for their son.

2. A returnee comes home to a party arranged by her family, relatives, and old friends. She is shocked to see how *they* have changed since they are wearing the latest fashions, doing the latest dances, and using the most current slang terms.

3. A Pacific Islander returns home and is faced with an ultimatum from his father: either he cuts his hair or he leaves the house.

4. Former participants are at a cocktail party with people who know little or nothing about Asia and the East-West Center. The cocktail chatter is filled with embarrassing pauses, nonsequiturs, ridiculous generalizations about Asians, and so forth. Finally, the participants and the other people break a previously arranged engagement with, "Well, I just remembered we have to do something else."

5. A female participant is being interviewed for a job by the boss of a small company. It becomes clear during the interview that the boss is interested in typing speed, not experiences with living and working with people from 40 countries; job experience, not ability to translate into Thai; and shorthand, not abstract knowledge of generative grammatical theory's generalizations to English language teaching.

E. ATTRIBUTION AND NONVERBAL BEHAVIOR

This is the single session that most clearly draws material from the social psychological literature. General notions of attribution theory are explained (Jones et al., 1972), especially two major findings: (1) People judge actions of others as being due to traits, but they are more likely to judge the same actions in themselves as being due to situational pressures: (2) People use extremely limited and sometimes faulty information in making trait inferences about others. This leads to a question for discussion: will people back home make trait judgments based on the behavior that they see in returnees, even though this information is limited? Will the trait inferences be negative (uppitty, too-Americanized, snobbish, know-it-all, etc.)?

This approach is similar to the culture assimilator work of Fiedler, Mitchell, and Triandis (1971) who also use specific and
critical incidents of this type to generate understanding of the
attribution process.

The emphasis on attributions made by others leads into
nonverbal behavior, for participants have often learned gestures common to other nationalities. A videotape on American
gestures is shown and the participants are asked, "Are you
bringing any back, and will there be problems because of it?"
For instance, Americans scratch the side of their head when
thinking about the answer to a difficult question, while Japanese scratch the top of their heads. The question for discussion:
What will people think if they see a Japanese returnee making
the quick American version of this nonverbal behavior? The
principle has already been presented that there will be a trait
inference from this inadequate piece of data, so the important
point is that there *will* be an inference. Other examples center
around the greater amount of bodily movement involved in
American as contrasted with Asian gestures, the differing dis-
tances people use in ordinary conversation across different
cultures (Sommer, 1969), and the fact of returnee-as-on-oddity
and thus the subject of much discussion by people back home.

F. MAINTAINING CROSS CULTURAL RELATIONS

This session contains the largest number of specific recommendations and is most unique to the special nature of the
East-West Center. The session is led by the alumni officer, who
tells about which East-West Center publications the participants will continue to receive, the different associations organized by former participants in the various countries, the
alumni directory, the occupations now held by former participants, the names of volunteers in various countries who will
help the new returnee join the alumni organizations, and so
forth. Generally, recommendations deal with maintaining ties
with people in the different countries and how to meet others
with similar international orientations. This session is scheduled last because it is uplifting, positive, and a relief after the
analysis of potential negative aspects of returning home.

Evaluation There have been five reorientations seminars
at the East-West Center (as of May, 1975). Evaluation has taken
the form of gathering participant response to the first pro-

gram, using this input to improve the second program, evaluating the second to improve the third, and so forth. This process is explained in Chapter four. In fact, the development of this approach to evaluation took place at the same time as the development of the reorientation seminar.

The measure of learning is simply the participants' answers to this question, completed before and after the program: "What problems do you think you might have after you return to your country? These might be any type of problem such as personal, family, job-related, and so forth." The results from answers to this question are likewise encouraging. The average number of answers (summarized for all programs to date) increased from one before the seminar to four after the seminar. This shows that participants are indeed learning and are becoming more cognitively complex in their thinking about the future. As an example, here are the exact answers from one participant. His preseminar answer to the question was

> I don't envisage any problem upon returning home as I already have a job waiting for me. There won't be any "cultural" shock either as I'm matured enough[3] to reorientate myself into the society from which I came. My only problem is mainly how to get myself acclimatized into the weather in my home country which is hot and humid!

After the stimulation of the seminar, however, he suggested a large number of potential problems in answer to the postprogram problem question:

1. Adjustment to humid and hot weather
2. Gifts to friends and relatives
3. Identification of his home environment and physical surroundings.
4. Psychological preparation against professional jealousy on the part of colleagues.

---

[3]The feeling that individual participants are so mature that they will have no readjustment problems comes up often. Because of this, we attempt to show that readjustment is a very normal process, and elements of it are encountered by virtually everyone. As mentioned previously, we often relate our own experiences to reinforce the notion that these issues are common to everyone.

5. Being prepared to living up to a graduate returning from a foreign country like the United States, as local people do expect a lot from him.

6. Re-establish relations with all friends at home.

7. Be aware of "too" Westernized behavior and attitudes picked up in the United States which might offend relatives and friends back home. Although all trainees did not increase to this marked degree, the average score shift from one to four shows the general trend in the direction of greater awareness of potential problems.

Some final comments. It would also be easy to argue, using exactly the data presented in this paper, that the staff of this program are causing returnees needless worry. Critics could point to the respondent who gave only one potential problem prior to the seminar but seven after, and they could say that ethical concerns come into question. The response is that the worry will be beneficial for many of the returnees because it will help them if problems actually do arise. Even if problems *do not* occur, the returnees who participate in the seminar will learn what *does* happen to a large number of people. One of the implicit assumptions of the East-West Center is that Asian, Pacific, and United States grantees will learn about the nature of people who have a multicultural orientation. One aspect of such people, of course, is the nature of the issues faced when they move from their home culture to another and back. Because of the seminar, participants have an opportunity (for the most part, their only formal opportunity) to learn about this process. This point became clear when a participant congratulated the staff on seminar and said, "I've learned so much. I never dreamed that there were all these things that can happen when people move from culture to culture. This has been a great educational experience."

In sum, the position is that a reorientation seminar can't lose. Some participants are helped through the worry-prepared method, and others have a unique opportunity to learn about multiculturality.

Intervention in Social Conflict

The most awe-inspiring attempts to apply cross-cultural orientation methods have been directed at bringing together recognized leaders of hostile factions within a given country, such as Northern Ireland or Cyprus. The hope of such meetings (most often referred to as workshops) is that new ideas for cooperation will be expressed, and that the members of the factions will get to know each other well enough that there will be contact across factions after the workshop. A small number of social scientists have become involved in these attempts at conflict resolution, and the person who has been most active is Leonard Doob. His work is referred to more often than that of others because he has written about his experiences and because the first author of this book has had a number of discussions with Doob about the intervention work. Doob (1975) published an overview of his work in a volume coedited by the first author.

Doob has been involved with the Fermeda workshop, designed to help solve border disputes in the Horn of Africa, which brought together representatives from Somalia, Ethiopia, and Kenya (Doob, 1970, 1971); the Belfast (also called Stirling) workshop, which brought together Catholics and Protestants from Northern Ireland (Doob and Foltz, 1973, 1974); and the unfortunately aborted Cyprus workshop, which was to bring together Greek and Turkish Cypriots (Doob, 1974). The latter had to be cancelled in the summer of 1974 because coups and invasions in Cyprus forced the evacuation of Professor Doob by the British Armed Forces and the American Sixth Fleet. These workshops were run (or were to be run) over a period of 10 to 13 days.

The problems involved in the planning, administration, and evaluation of these programs are enormous, as Doob freely admits and explains carefully so that anyone else wishing to attempt the same sort of activity can benefit from his experiences. In these workshops one goal is to choose participants who have influence in the communities from which they come, who are creative and open-minded as possible, and who might be able to put some of the workshop suggestions into

practice after they return home. Finding such people is difficult. Doob has been able to recruit interested and strategically
located individuals in the countries in which he has worked,
and he has been able to secure nominations for participants
from high-level officials (in Cyprus, from people at very high
levels). Doob cautions that the disadvantage of working with
in-country colleagues is that they can be left "holding the bag,"
if anything goes wrong after "the screwball, do-gooder American professor has gone back to his cushy job at Yale."[4] Another
selection problem involves the final choice of the people nomi-
nated. In the Cyprus case (Doob, 1974) the planning had gone
so well for the proposed workshop that the concept had
achieved a good deal of acceptance. Consequently, those not
chosen became angry and perhaps might have formed a core
of opponents to ideas generated by those who *were* chosen for
the workshop.

Funding is difficult. Explaining the problem as "chicken-
and-egg," Doob (1974) points out that funding agencies do not
want to sponsor a workshop unless it is feasible and desirable,
and yet organizers cannot be sure of feasibility and desirability
(or even possibility, since potential participants will want to
know if it's a "real thing") until they are sure of financial support. It has been difficult to obtain the informed consent of the
potential participants, that is, to let them know what will happen and at the same time persuade them to participate. Because so few workshops of this type have been held, it is almost
impossible to predict what will happen. It is also difficult to
convey the possibility that nothing much of any good will happen in solving a country's problems, which, after all, is one
possible outcome of a workshop. A major problem is the possibility that workshop participants will be held suspect after
they return home, since they have just recently interacted
with members of the other faction. Will their credibility in
their community be destroyed as a result of their participation? In the planning of the workshops Doob (1974, 1975) has
recommended the same sorts of practical guidelines that we
cover in Chapter five. Doob makes special pleas that work-

---

[4]We hope it is obvious that we are using the possible language of disappointed and
angry participants, and that we are not expressing our own feelings.

shops be held at a significant distance from the participants' home base, and that there be a organization element to handle administrative details so that the interveners are allowed to do their job. We cover both these points in the planning and administration of any cross-cultural orientation program.

Once the participants are at the conference site, the techniques used are not different from the ones we have already reviewed, although the content of the discussions, role-plays, and the like may be more volatile than average. Doob (1975) reviewed six possibilities: (1) lectures, (2) meetings, or group discussions, with a specific topic to be discussed, (3) games or simulations, such as role-playing, (4) observations of one another during confrontations, (5) group methods, in which people are encouraged to work with one another and to discover how groups function, and (6) interviewing, or direct questioning of the participants (by the interveners) to determine their attitudes, feelings, and perceived facts about the conflict. A concept that we were surprised to see not reviewed (one of us contributed to a discussion of this omission: Brislin, Bochner, and Lonner, 1975) is the search for superordinate goals (Sherif, 1958). These are goals that would be valued by both groups, but which demand the joint efforts of both groups to achieve them. Sherif (1958, 1967) has indicated how striving for such goals can reduce intergroup tension and conflict. In a personal communication, however, Doob indicates that there is indeed a search for such goals, but he prefers not to use the term coined by Sherif. Of the methods he suggests, Doob has used all except interviewing, and he prefers the types of techniques to which we have given the most attention in this book, such as role-playing, group discussions, planning for activities after the workshop, and active involvement in the actual program at the workshop.

Goals of workshops can be general (e.g., help solve the conflict by encouraging the generation of new ideas) or specific (e.g., in Cyprus, encourage the development of history texts that feature the contributions of both Greek and Turkish people). Evaluation data are extremely difficult to obtain, because the assessment of a control group of similar influential people, who do not participate in a workshop, is nearly impossible to obtain. Doob and Foltz (1974) interviewed members of the Belfast workshop 9 months after their participation, and the members reported enthusiasm for the workshop. Some members indicated modest success in their carrying out of plans they developed at the conference. The preparation for re-entry into the home community after the workshop has not received a great deal of attention, although we were pleased when Doob told us that one of the few scholarly papers he took with him to Cyprus was a preprint of our materials on re-entry cross-cultural programs.

The workshop-intervention concept has not achieved acceptance from all behavioral and social scientists, or from members of committees involved in the planning and administration of the workshops. Reacting to the Belfast workshop, four critics from Northern Ireland (Boehringer, Zeroulis, Bayley, and Boehringer, 1974, pp. 274–275) wrote, based on the first-hand experiences of two of them:

> . . . . It is our feeling that the goals of the exercise were confused and unsubstantiated either theoretically or practically and that this confusion allowed for serious errors of judgment regarding the political and ethical propriety of the exercise. All this is somewhat disguised by the haphazard nature of the research methodology which makes evaluation more a matter of guesswork than anything else.
>
> Furthermore, we believe that it could not have taken place without the prevalence of the "mandarin" attitude among many conflict researchers. It is this attitude that allows for intervention into the lives of ordinary people on the basis of insufficient theory and without regard to human cost. Furthermore, the use of "scientific" language and the glamour of professionalism gains admittance to a dazzled community on the basis of a relationship, that is, to say the least, asymmetrical. It is our feeling that fruitful work can be based only on a more honest, open relationship with the people with whom one works . . .

Doob and Foltz responded (in Alevy et al., 1974, p. 284):

> .... the [Belfast] Workshop sought not just to do research, and not at all to experiment on people, but to teach and train community leaders about group and intergroup processes so that they would be able to function more effectively from their own standpoint when they returned to their communities.
>
> The Workshop experience was an important event in the lives of the 56 participants and 9 staff members. It could doubtless have benefited from better planning and better follow-up, but it would be naive to blame any deficiencies exclusively on the administrators, organizers, or consultants. All of us remained through the Stirling phase and are therefore responsible in our different roles for the learning and nonlearning that took place there. The stress experienced at Stirling can be made to look like a shortsighted mistake or an invaluable opportunity for growth and learning. We expect that over time the learning will prevail.

This exchange should give an indication of the sorts of reactions interveners *will* (not *are likely to*) receive in carrying out their work. When activities as daring, complex, and audacious as intervention workshops are attempted, such work will draw criticism like magnets draw metal—criticism is absolutely inevitable! Just as in an analysis through the worry-prepared method or taking advantage of the positive effects yielded by an examination of a problem's troublesome aspects, it is important for potential interveners to foresee the negative reactions they will receive. But we are unable to summarize such work better than Doob (1974, p. 177);

> In a single, compound sentence: it is possible for one person with patience and time, with adequate financial support, with the promise of the possibility of continued support, and with assistance from local associates and back-home colleagues to intervene in a conflict situation and to organize a workshop; the satisfactions, the risks, and the disappointment can be great.

Effectiveness of Techniques Found within Larger Programs

The training programs reviewed thus far are almost always composed of several techniques, and these techniques have been studied by social psychologists interested in attitude change. Although these researchers have not always dealt with cross-cultural training, their findings are applicable to such instruction.

1. *Guided reading.* Vassiliou et al. (1968) tested the intercultural attitudes of 62 Americans living in Greece after they read an essay about the Greek culture. Knowledge about Greece increased, but intercultural attitudes did not improve. This finding will not surprise investigators who feel that more active effort than reading an essay is necessary for attitude change.

This study is particularly important for its application to business and industry. A common practice is to give people books or pamphlets about other countries. The above study indicates that even if these are read, there may be no increase in favorable feelings toward members of that country. If the purpose is to convey *content* rather than *feeling*, guided reading (where there are insurances that the material is studied) seems useful. But if the purpose is to change feelings or attitudes, a more active procedure is necessary. The criticism does not apply to programmed reading materials, such as the cultural assimilator, which demand active participation.

2. *Equal status contact between groups.* Amir (1969) has reviewed a great deal of literature and has concluded that the following often-heard notion is true: pleasant contact between ethnic groups, in an equal-status situation, increases favorable attitudes. The point to be remembered, however, is that the separate elements in this principle must be in effect; that is, the contact must be pleasant *and* the groups must meet in an equal-status relation (one group, especially the majority group, cannot have more power or be able to receive more rewards than the other). Especially effective contact occurs when the members of the groups engage in interdependent activity to achieve a goal that is desired by all concerned (Sherif, 1958).

In a well-designed experimental work program, Cook

(1970) provided highly prejudiced white subjects with pleasant and equal-status contact with a black co-worker. Whites viewed the interaction as part of their work (for which they were paid). After 20 days of such interaction (2 hours a day), a large number of the white subjects had changed their attitudes. Cook is continuing his work in this area, and his future efforts will undoubtedly yield increased insight into situations where intergroup contact leads to positive effects.

The point about equal-status contact has applicability to cross-cultural programs that have foreign nationals as members of the training staff, and with programs that encourage contact with host nationals. Contact either within or outside training must take place under the proper circumstances.

3. *Group discussion.* Lewin (1947) reviewed several studies showing changes in behavior that took place after group discussion. During World War II meat was scarce, and officials thought that the shortage problem might be lessened if housewives would use more beef hearts, sweetbreads, and kidneys. Lewin and his associates set up an experiment in which some housewives participated in group discussion and some received a lecture about this desired change. A nutrition expert gave the lecture and was available for comment in the discussion group. Follow-up interviews at 2- and 4-week intervals showed that the housewives who had participated in the group discussions were serving more of the recommended foods than the housewives who had heard the lecture. Based on her own research, Bennet (1955) pointed out that the influential factors in the group discussion were probably: (1) the housewives came to a decision, and (2) they perceived that others came to the same decision.

Coch and French (1948) studied worker productivity after a change had been made in the style of pajamas their company produced. The sewing machine operators were divided into three groups. One group was simply told of the change and told what to do. Another group elected representatives to help decide what would be done to effect the change. A third group participated totally, through discussion, in deciding the best way to go about making the necessary changes. Over 30 days the total-participation groups produced more units than the others. The participation-through-representation group produced more than the no-participation group. This latter group actually declined in production when compared to their performance before the experiment started.

These results indicate that group discussion is a valuable technique and that it can be used in a wide variety of situations, as long as group members know something about the subject matter under discussion (Kerrick et al., 1967).

4. *Role playing.* In this book we have noted several times that the purpose of cross-cultural training is to induce long-range effects on a person's behavior toward foreign nationals. The follow-up studies, however, have rarely studied behavior more than 2 to 4 weeks after an attitude change program. To determine the long-range effects of such techniques as role-playing, the non-cross-cultural literature must be studied.

Role-playing studies have been reviewed by Elms (1967, 1972). A noteworthy series of studies are those of Janis and Mann (1965) and Mann and Janis (1968). In the first study, heavy smokers role-played a cancer patient in a very emotional scenario. Another group of subjects listened to a role-play confrontation between a patient and doctor which had been taped. The 1968 study provided data on the subjects' smoking behavior 18 months after the experiment. The role-play subjects reported the least amount of smoking. The listen-to-tape group also had cut down, but not as much as role-players. A control group which had received no treatment did not change at all.

The role-playing technique was effective because of its emotion-arousing nature; one conclusion from the research is that to be effective, role playing must engage the emotions of the participants (it can't be dull and lifeless!). A role-play subject reported (also commenting on the Surgeon General's report linking smoking and health) the following to an opinion pollster long after her role play experience:

> The (Surgeon General's) report did not have much effect on me. But I was in this other study. A professor was doing this psychological thing and I was one of the volunteers. And that was what really affected me. . . . He was the one that scared

me, not the report . . . I got to thinking, what if it were really true and I had to go home and tell everyone that I had cancer. And right then I decided I would not go through this again, and if there were any way of preventing it I would. And I stopped smoking. It was really the professor's study that made me quit (Mann and Janis, 1968, p. 342).

These studies have several direct applications to cross-cultural training. First, the Intercultural Communication Workshop and the Reorientation Seminars have, as part of their content, a role-play situation in which one trainee acts in a scenario with an instructor and a large audience watches. The role-playing often arouses emotion. According to the Janis–Mann studies, both the role players and the audience should learn from this method.

Second, an unexpected finding of the Janis–Mann studies was that both role players and listeners were more receptive (in their behavior) to the recommendations of the Surgeon General's report, even if they did not admit it, than untreated control subjects. That is, the report had an effect on the role-players and listeners, but not on people who had not had these experiences. Perhaps role-playing in cross-cultural instruction can prepare trainees to be receptive to written materials, which they can then read under supervision.

Training Programs and Their Desirable Aspects: Summary

In the first chapter we listed a number of factors that should be found in a good cross-cultural training program. In this summary section we would like to repeat that list, add other items to it, and point out which programs just reviewed constitute good examples of each factor. This will serve the dual purpose of highlighting the desirable aspects of certain programs and emphasizing the large number of factors that have to be a part of a good program.

1. A program should have researchable goals. The culture assimilator studies, the program reviewed under the title of "The Army's alien presence," and the in-service training pro-

gram all have in common the specific, well-defined goal of teaching people from one culture (in these cases, most attention has been given to Americans from the middle class) how to interact, get along, work effectively, and cause as few communication difficulties as possible with members of another cultural group. This is a researchable goal because empirical data can confirm or disconfirm that a program is providing such skills.

2. Assumptions should be based on data. In our review or existing programs, this is the factor that we feel has been most commonly met. As some examples, the culture assimilator work, the programs involving case studies, and the simulation design assume that certain problem areas should be included in training. Their assumptions are based on data because program directors discovered the problem areas (also called critical incidents) by interviewing people in cross-cultural situations who have to face such problems on a day-to-day basis. These people include both members of the culture who are to undergo training and the members of the host culture who "put up with" members of the culture about to undergo training.

3. Combine selection and training. Many people who have been involved in cross-cultural training feel that there is more benefit to be gained from selecting people who can interact effectively in other cultures than there is in attempting to train people who may not be predisposed to ever go very far beyond the background of their first culture. Whatever the merits of this argument, it seems clear that if selection of people for cross-cultural training can be done in conjunction with training, there will be greater benefit than if either is attempted alone. The program we call the cross-cultural interaction design gives explicit attention to this meshing of selection and training and is worthy of careful study.

4. Draw ideas from a variety of other programs. Many program directors will be eclectic in designing their own programs, drawing good ideas from wherever they can be found. The Intercultural Communication Workshop is a good example. It includes the elements of role-playing, readings, critical incidents, and communication exercises, all of which have

been shown to be effective teaching methods.

5. Provide social support for the types of behavior recommended during training. This point emphasizes the fact that the purpose of training is to encourage favorable cross-cultural interaction not only during the training program, but long after the program has ceased. The life-skills model is a good example because it provides opportunities to try out skills learned during training "in the real world, and to then share experiences with other participants back in the training environment. The reorientation seminar we reviewed contains an entire session devoted to telling participants how they might meet others with similar experiences. The point to be remembered is that a given set of behaviors is more likely to occur, on the part of a given individual, when everyone else in the environment is also engaging in the behaviors, because there is so much social support. Models who can show how to engage in the favorable behaviors should be part of the training program. It would also be desirable if people (with whom the program participants are likely to have contact) who have a reputation for engaging in favorable behaviors toward people of other cultures could be identified. Program participants could then see how the principles of training work in the everyday lives of certain model individuals.

6. Provide transfer of training to the real world. Techniques should exist to show how to use knowledge gained during training, in contrast to presenting principles in the abstract without a "how to do it" component. The shore-leave exchange program teaches specific skills or brings a group together who have similar interests. The program director then tells the trainees exactly where and how to exploit these skills and interests in the host culture. In general, any program with a role-playing component satisfies this desirable factor, because the trainee has to learn a great deal about another culture, or people in the other culture, if he or she is to present an effective and realistic role-play scenario.

7. Determine how much learning is retained. The self-confrontation and Contrast-American techniques measure how much material from training is remembered. In the self-confrontation research, learning was measured 2 weeks from

training, and in the Contrast-American studies learning was measured 23 months after training. The longer time span is, of course, the more desirable.

8. Replicate major findings. The culture assimilator, self-confrontation technique, and reorientation seminar have all been subjected to a series of evaluative studies. Such replication allows researchers to determine if the program holds up to frequent evaluation rather than to a one-shot study.

9. Evaluate training, not only by asking trained people about the other culture under study, but also by asking people from the culture under study about those who have undergone training. Part of the program reviewed under "The Army's Alien Presence" contains this element. After the training took place in Korea, Koreans were asked what they think of Americans. Because the purpose of training is to encourage favorable cross-cultural interaction, the hosts' perception of the visitors is certainly an important measure. In many cases the Koreans did not know which Americans received training; thus their answers were not contaminated by this knowledge.

10. Evaluate the behavior of trained people toward members of other cultures. Explicit attention to this point shows recognition of the fact that the purpose of training is not only to encourage favorable attitudes, but also favorable behaviors. Unfortunately, no studies have been done on behavior evaluation.

11. Programs should be evaluated by people unassociated (having no vested interest) with the program. In one study of the culture assimilator, the criterion was the supervisor's rating of the trainee's effectiveness. These supervisors had no vested interest in whether the culture assimilator was good or bad, and probably did not know which of the people had received training.

The factors involved in our discussion of points 9 to 11 will be expanded in Chapter four.

12. Provide follow-up training. In the best programs, the participants meet after the training program so that progress can be discussed. A very good example can be found in Arnold's (1967) summary of a Peace Corps program in which volunteers in a certain area came together frequently to share

problems, as well as to socialize. The wisdom of this follow-up training was shown by the archival records showing fewer premature returns to the United States on the part of the Peace Corps volunteers in this area.

The number of factors involved in a good program is admittedly large, yet, the number of problems which the programs are designed to overcome is even larger.

CHAPTER

4

POTENTIAL AUDIENCES FOR
CROSS-CULTURAL ORIENTATION PROGRAMS

Multinational Corporations

The majority of training programs for multinational corporations have evolved independently of each other without adequate lines of communication between sponsors. Likewise, the various programs have developed their own criteria of effectiveness, resulting in considerable confusion. The majority of the programs for preparing development technicians fail to treat all essential curriculum areas. Many of the curriculum areas and skills that are presented are frequently regarded as meaningless by the participating technicians. Finally, the curriculum and skills covered in training programs based in the United States are often not in agreement with those that would be covered by persons in the field.

The literature suggests the need to coordinate training programs for multinational corporations. First, training must recognize that there is a problem and that traditional methods have been inadequate to meet the need. Innovative attempts to incorporate human relations workshops, intercultural training, and organized programs have shown limited development in the right direction. Second, training personnel need to be able to recognize failure when it occurs. Third, the problems that inhibit intercultural adjustment need to be examined more closely and in greater detail, rather than as generalized abstractions. Fourth, efforts to conceptualize problems in an analytical framework allow application of basic behavioral science research. Fifth, there is a need to look at the methods of educational training that have proven successful in other areas on parallel tasks. Finally, the field of training needs to develop new programs.

Bass (1969) described a data bank at the Management Research Center, University of Rochester to collect and disseminate cross-cultural information relating to Americans abroad and their relation to host nationals. Such a bank would assist in overcoming the misunderstanding and resistance to change described by Triandis (1967) between Americans and host nationals. The data bank has focused on how Americans and host nationals react to the same standardized intercultural incidents. The persons who have been studied are middle or senior managers from governmental, military and industrial areas. The data are collected through a "Program of Exercises for Management and Organizational Development" that simulates key management activities. Each trainee makes a decision on which solution would be appropriate to the decision. Next, he meets with a small group to discuss the situation, and the group makes a decision. The individual and group decisions are compared with other groups and individuals completing the same tasks to provide direct feedback. The work of this project is carried out through the International Research Group on Management (IRGOM), the European Research Group on Management (ERGOM), CINSELA in Latin America, MITRA in India, NIRGOM in Japan, and NARGOM in North America.

On the basis of his findings Bass (1969) has found both universal and culturally unique elements in managerial style. On the basis of his data Bass has developed a model of translational understanding that describes eight situations of understanding and misunderstanding. In this model four situations occur when the American advisor and host national are actually *similar* in values, attitudes, or behavior and when.

1. Both see the similarities.

2. The American sees differences; the host sees differences; the host sees the similarities.

3. The American sees the similarities; the host sees differences.

4. Both see differences. Likewise, four situations occur when the American advisor and the host national are actually different in values, attitudes, or behavior.

1. Both perceive themselves as similar.

2. The American accurately sees the difference, but the host perceives similarity.

3. The host accurately sees differences, but the American perceives similarity.

4. Both perceive themselves as different. When both partners perceive accurately represents situations of least conflict due to a misunderstanding of one another. Each relationship applies its own combination of constraints and opportunities. Data can be classified from training programs in which members of different nationalities are assembled in the same program, responding to the same simulated exercises. On the basis of this data, training programs can be designed and refined on specific patterns of culture-related behaviors. Coordinated training would provide group as well as individual responses which could be related to other relevant indicators.

Hitchin (1968) pointed out that many difficulties faced by the international manager relates to the home office and not to the manager abroad, however well he may or may not be trained. To the extent that the corporate officials are responsible for making decisions, they must also be aware of how cultural differences influence operations. Managers abroad are in a difficult position. They must represent the host country to the domestic company, negotiating benefits to both the company and the host country, while interpreting each side's point of view to the other! As Stewart (1969) pointed out, efforts in training for cross-cultural interaction should be linked to analyses of the organizations in which the trained persons will work. The relationship between the individual and his work group is integral to training, with the *company* needing training in the role of multinationalism as much as the individual. The primary question is perhaps not the training of individuals but organizing work and social activities to liberate cultural differences as resources rather than suppressing them as obstacles to cross-cultural communication and cooperation. Each multinational corporation needs to become more aware of how culturally determined attitudes, values, and judgments affect their business administrative practices.

There is a commonly held but dangerous assumption in business that a capable executive in the United States will soon learn the language, customs, and skills of adaptation to a foreign country. Consistent with this assumption, and given the limited time available between selection and foreign placement, predeparture training would seem to be a luxury no company can afford. Dickerman and Davis (1966) surveyed overseas managerial programs and discovered that few had any systematic intercultural training program. There has been progress, however, since Hodgson (1961) discovered that only three out of seventy large United States corporations gave predeparture training. In a more recent study of predeparture training, Ivancevich (1969) reported that about 33 percent of the 127 firms surveyed offered some form of predeparture preparation.

In a study of the curricula in that training, preparation in the nation's customs and language are considered the most valuable topics for adjusting to the host country. A large number of areas were not considered sufficiently important to be included. When the managers were asked to rate these areas according to their importance, training in the host country language was considered the most valuable, and discussion of the religions in that host country were considered to be least important. Training in the living conditions, economics, and customs of the host nation were all rated as having considerable value.

On the basis of his data, Ivancevich (1969) recommended that managers who have already worked abroad could best teach in the training programs. Programs covering issues specific to a given country could be developed by educational institutions with specialized expertise in the field for part of the training. As a model he cites the program of the Business Council of International Understanding at the American University School of International Service whose curriculum includes techniques of representing the employer overseas; the study of national differences; analysis of economic, labor, political, and social facts of life; area study; private consultations with foreign specialists; orientation of wives; and language study.

American multinational corporations have been in business for decades, but with the formation of the European Common Market in 1958 the growth of America's multinationals was greatly increased with an estimated $75 billion invested in Western Europe alone. The reason for wholesale transfer of capital to Europe resulted from the discovery that American corporations could buy more for their overvalued dollar in Europe than they could at home, making it cheaper to produce in Europe than to export from America. With the devaluation of the dollar we have begun to experience a reversal of that trend with more foreign multinational companies coming to the United States.

Pressure from protectionists has restricted the movement of American capital abroad. Growing nationalism abroad has also inhibited American technological domination as the foreign corporations have become more competitive. Foreign countries have begun to tighten restrictions on American investments and to protect their own industries. In the ebb and flow of world economics, the one certainty is that corporations around the world are becoming more multinational in their search for a market. This trend will certainly require larger numbers of trained personnel and more adequate methods of training them.

Government Agencies

The role of technical experts abroad is compounded by the same problems confronting every foreigner abroad, namely, the definition of their task by the sponsoring agency, the experts own view of their role, the knowledge skills and action required by their job, and receptivity by a host culture. They are often confounded by communications with the host country, on one hand, and their back-home agencies, on the other. Technical cooperation operations abroad tend to exaggerate differences between line and staff responsibilities, with the back-home agency functioning in its own culture and administrative milieu while the foreign expert must adapt to a quite different set of circumstances. Success abroad depends heavily on receptivity by the host country toward technical cooperation, with a different system of constraints operative in each national setting, for each technical function. The host country must perceive a need for the expert's services before they are likely to accept them (Goodenough, 1963).

Haines (1964) visited a number of government agencies and research organizations and asked what problems they have in preparing Americans for work with indigenous personnel overseas. Each agency was asked about the goal of their training program, the curriculum of that program, the methods used in teaching, and the problems faced by trainees in achieving those goals. The first goal was a rapid and effective training in cross-cultural skills that would prevent "Ugly American" incidents abroad. However comprehensive the training program, it could still do more harm than good without adequate cross-cultural skills in communication concerning the significant difference between knowing the theory of what should be done and being actually able to carry it out.

Until after World War II, no systematic overseas training existed for the professional Foreign Service Officers of the United States. It was not until the passage of the Foreign Service Act of 1946 that problems of recruitment and training of foreign service personnel were systematically dealt with. The act of 1946 established the Foreign Service Institute, based on the division of training service that had been set up in the State Department. Visits with experts who had recently returned from foreign areas were substituted for systematic study about foreign cultures. Language training was usually left to the technician's own energy and initiative. Until the late 1950s officers assigned to the Military Assistance Advisory Groups, responsible for administering $2 or $3 billion worth of military aid a year, received no special training at all. Campbell (1969) summarized the programs used for training the military for overseas assignments, and Foster (1969) outlined the needs and task analysis for cross-cultural training. The emphasis on programs modeled after Peace Corps training and accelerated research by the military have contributed greatly to the development of more adequate programs. It is still true, however, that such an obvious cross-cultural agency as the Immigration and Naturalization Service does not train its staff beyond acquainting them with the agency's own internal organization, almost completely disregarding the cultural values of their prospective clientele.

The Foreign Service Institute, Center for Area and Country Studies Washington, D.C., does most of the cross-cultural training for the State Department and for other government agencies requesting assistance. Information on their programs is available on request. The Navy has recently contracted with the Center for Research and Education in Denver, Colorado to develop cross-cultural orientation programs mentioned elsewhere in this book. The Human Resources Research Organization connected with American University has also developed a large amount of specific training materials for government agencies. Finally Department of State *Background Notes* are available through the U.S. Government Printing Office.

The problems of political involvement and confidentiality are particularly complicated for cross-cultural training of government personnel. Some of the materials are necessarily classified and administratively complicated to obtain. Furthermore, when the personnel reach their field assignment, they are forced to cope with hostility toward a policy or attitude toward their government with which they might not even agree as individuals but must represent and even defend as part of their job. The suspicion of their ties with agencies such as the Central Intelligence Agency are even more likely to confound their adjustment to a foreign country and acceptance by local nationals. The special problems of cross-cultural adjustment are extremely difficult for government personnel, who require additional orientation beyond the training required for nongovernment personnel going abroad.

The government orientation programs for foreign nationals coming to this country are perhaps even less sensitive than those of educational institutions and industry in helping trainees adjust to communication difficulties when entering a new culture. Sinauer (1967) is very critical of the government orientation programs and advocates a transition seminar for foreign nationals coming to the United States. Such an orientation seminar would incorporate the learning of English with the broader problems of how to communicate in a foreign country.

Foreign Students in the United States

The assumptions that have supported foreign student programs in American universities have generally related either to our national "obligation" to less developed countries or to an opportunity for broadening the scope of local students through exposure to persons from other countries. There has been very little serious effort to incorporate the unique resources foreign students—many of whom are high-ranking in their own universities back home—bring into an academic community. Eide (1970) lists the more commonly accepted assumptions as (1) that more knowledge about another culture leads to more empathy, sympathy, and, ultimately, improved intercultural relations, (2) that acquaintance with other cultures will result in increased tolerance, (3) that culture sharing will result in a synthesis of cultures, interdependence, and exchange of resources to everyone's mutual advantage, and (4) that intercultural exchange will clarify our knowledge about ourselves. The international community on our university campuses provides a valuable resource for cross-cultural orientation in both formal and nonformal programs of international education.

The Institute of International Education's annual publication *Open Doors* estimates that 151,000 foreign students were studying in the United States in 1973–1974, although their estimates are generally considered about 20 percent below the actual number (Semas, 1975). Looking at those statistics we may conclude "there is no foreign student" when we consider the extreme diversity of cultures, fields, ages, and demographic data about this extremely diverse population. The only shared characteristic is their being in the United States on a study program temporarily. In the first comprehensive description of foreign students studying in the United States, Glasser (1975) researched the phenomena of foreign student's migration to the United States and eventual decision about whether to stay in the United States or return home. The few studies on foreign students after they have returned to their home country are reviewed by Bochner (1973), in an empirical study of East West Center students.

In the last 5 years enrollments of foreign students have increased by 30,000 persons (Semas, 1975), with every indication that the larger increases are still to come. Many of the universities, facing declining enrollments by American students, are actively recruiting foreign students who have funding from locations such as Hong Kong, where English is widely spoken, or from the oil-producing nations. Although many of the smaller, private schools seeking foreign student undergraduates do not intend to be unethical, they are not equipped to deal with problems and opportunities of international cultural exchange. Quite aside from problems of cultural adjustment described in this book, many of these colleges lack a full-time foreign student advisor, an internationally experienced admissions officer, and the procedures for orienting foreign students and handling the complicated legal requirements. The unfortunate result of an inadequately planned program is more foreign students returning home to positions of considerable power and authority with deep resentments and and misunderstandings about the United States. There is evidence that foreign students returning home are frequently more negative in their opinion of the United States when they leave than when they first came (Yeh & Chu, 1974, Torrey et al., 1970).

An examination of the literature on foreign students in the United States leads to the conclusion that we could do a much more adequate job in this area. A frequent complaint of foreign students is that Americans are initially friendly but that this friendship is superficial or even insincere, preventing the establishment of many deep friendships. The adjustment process no doubt inhibits close relationships in ways that could be minimized through more effective orientation of both the foreign students and the Americans. Moran et al. (1974) describe an orientation program design in which faculty, community persons, host families, and old *and* new foreign students are brought together in a retreat setting to orient one another in an exchange of information and insights. Orientation should certainly not be limited to the newcomer foreign students, but should include all persons interacting in the international university community as a unit. The language problem is certainly another factor inhibiting close personal relations within the international university community. Pedersen (1975a) suggests a previously untried approach in organizing problem-specific nondegree programs in languages other than English for groups of foreign students from non-English-speaking countries who would be taught by any faculty or upper-level graduate students available to teach those topics in the student's national language. The foreign student is most likely to rely on other foreign students and fellow countrymen for help on personal problems. In situations in which a faculty advisor understands the student's culture or in which there is a high level of internationalism in the curricula or student activities, they would go outside their own foreign student community for help on personal problems (Pedersen, 1975b).

In response to the special problems of foreign students, the National Association for Foreign Student Affairs (NAFSA) was organized in 1948 to coordinate foreign student advisors and, more recently, foreign students as participating members. In the area of cross-cultural training NAFSA has developed a field service program which organizes many activities. It arranges, upon request, institutional consultations to review and recommend possible improvements in foreign student advising, teaching of English as a second language, admissions, procedures, and community services. It provides in-service training grants. It organizes and subsidizes special problem workshops. It gives travel grants to enable persons to attend

national and regional conferences. It runs a substantial publications program of guides and instruction manuals covering
the major activities of advising foreign students.

Some of the larger concentrations of foreign students are
served by residential living-learning centers such as the International Houses at Berkeley, New York, and Chicago. Other
more elaborate orientation programs for foreign students have
provided opportunities for cross-cultural exchange with
Americans through the Fulbright Program and the Institute of
International Education. Some of the larger universities provide host families of United States nationals or brother-sister
programs to encourage the informal exchange of insights between cultures. At the East-West Center, in Honolulu, students from the United States, Asia, and the Pacific interact in
a variety of formal or informal training programs while working on degree programs at the University of Hawaii.

Cross-cultural training of foreign students has usually
been limited to problems that impede communication and
cooperation. In reality, the same cultural differences have a
potential also to enhance an individual's understanding both of
his own and an alternative world view. From the point of view
of cross-cultural training, therefore, the most interesting environment is the one in which several cultural traditions come
into contact with one another in a setting where neither tradition is assimilated. Useem et al. (1963) cited the example of
"bi-national third culturals," or complex patterns of sharing
and learning in communities containing both Western and
non-Western traditions. The experience of a sojourner "foreign" student in a university community has provided us with
considerable insight into third culture alternatives through
research on the temporary means-oriented adjustment and
adaptation of students from other parts of the world.

A functional acculturation by foreign students requires
that they develop new skills in both on- and off-campus relationships which promote their progress along the continuum
of adjustment. In their off-campus relationships foreign students preserve their own identity and protect themselves
against the "foreign" culture in a variety of ways. Although the

quality of foreign students interaction with their hosts is described by Gezi (1965) as a very significant factor in the student's adjustment, other research by Klein et al. (1971) suggest that we overestimate the value of person-to-person contact between visitors and hosts and under-estimate the importance of interaction with co-nationals. Herman and Schild (1961) and recently Antler (1970) also concluded that the amount of interaction with fellow countrymen was of greater importance in their adjustment than interaction with Americans. Functional differences in social customs and peer-group social contacts provide almost insurmountable barriers to cross-cultural contact. Research among Chinese students at the University of Wisconsin demonstrated three implications of this behavior.

1. International students associate mostly with fellow nationals because warm, intimate, dependent, personally satisfying contacts are almost exclusively limited to their co-national group.

2. Their relations with host-country nationals rarely go beyond superficial pleasantries.

3. They are frequently discouraged about any prospects for deep cross-cultural friendships and do not expect such friendships to develop. The result is almost a "paranoid" attitude toward the hosts which tends to increase over time. (Yeh & Chu, 1974).

In the Selltiz (1963) study of 300 students from many countries at 34 United States colleges, about 70 percent of the students indicated that close friendships or going out socially with Americans were infrequent or rare events. Even though about half the students indicated that they spent much of their free time with Americans, another 50 percent indicated that they never spoke with Americans as they would with a close friend from home. The evidence continues to accumulate that more effective programs of cross-cultural orientation are necessary in our universities across the country, not only to prevent problems and misunderstandings that are sure to arise, but also to utilize more efficiently the tremendous opportunity for intercultural education provided by the presence of foreign student groups in our institutions of higher learning.

United States Students and Faculty Abroad

More United States students were reported abroad in 1970–1971 than have ever been recorded previously. All the students reported were regularly enrolled students in foreign university-level institutions. These figures may, therefore, be considered conservative, both because of reporting difficulties and because of the students who may be connected with foreign universities but not formally registered.

In 1970 more than half of the 30,000 United States students were studying in Europe (55%), as has been the case previously, followed by North America (16%), Latin America (15%), the Far East (7%), the Near and Middle East (5%), and Africa (1%). The distribution of their fields of study were likewise concentrated, with 39 percent in the humanities, 12 percent in medical sciences, 12 percent in social sciences, 4 percent in physical and life sciences, 2 percent in business administration, 2 percent in education, 1 percent in engineering, 1 percent in agriculture, and 29 percent in other fields.

There are many advantages to study abroad that contribute to a liberal arts education. The most obvious advantage is to give the United States student increased competence in a foreign language. A second advantage is exposure to a different country and international affairs through first-hand involvement. A third advantage is to gain more knowledge and appreciation of the student's own cultural heritage. The student can, therefore, expect to gain a better understanding of at least one foreign country, a better understanding of one's own culture, and a sense of personal growth.

There are at least five types of overseas experiences that constitute international training.

1. The IIE publication *Study Abroad* lists degree programs conducted by foreign universities and institutions.

2. A number of universities have organized short-term study tours with an academic emphasis for credit when a group of United States students travel with a faculty member.

3. Low-cost travel programs are operated by organizations such as the National Student Association, the American Youth Hostels, and a number of university programs.

4. Hospitality programs are available in which participants spend almost the entire summer in one country living with a host family. Intercultural Student Experiences, Inc., centered in Minnesota, provides credit experiences for secondary school language classes, in which the members go abroad during the school year. The language experience is accompanied by an extensive orientation preparation curricula.

5. Work camp programs are conducted by many voluntary associations such as the American Friends Service Committee, Operation Crossroads Africa, Ecumenical Voluntary Service, and others appealing to young people motivated toward social service.

The Experiment in International Living's School for International Training at Brattleboro, Vermont, established in 1964, is a multinational university with the motto "by living together, people learn to live together." In addition to offering courses leading toward a Masters degree, the Experiment is best known for its independent study programs in which a group of 8 to 10 students and an academic director spend a semester in another culture, with about 150 to 200 students representing more than 80 different institutions participate each semester. Each program includes an orientation program, language study, a home-stay, a contemporary culture seminar, and an independent study project. Chapman College in Orange, California operates the World Campus Afloat where an ocean liner is chartered for cruises up to a semester in length. Classes are taught aboard ship, and as the ship puts into foreign ports aspects of that host culture are worked into the curriculum. The objective is to provide students with direct first-hand experience among nationals from other cultures as part of their academic experience. Washington International Center in Washington, D. C. has just initiated a three-phase project directed toward developing model orientation programs and materials for international education and communication under the direction of Edward Stewart. The cultural unit of the State Department, who are funding this project, are intending to coordinate some of the otherwise diverse resources in the field of study abroad. Fieg and Blair (1975) published a collection of 12 intercultural perspectives from comments by foreign students and visitors about specific peculiarities of Americans from their own cultural viewpoints. Also, opportunities exist for individuals to travel abroad on their own without connection to any institutional program. The U.S. Department of Health, Education, and Welfare (1972) has provided a resource guide for American students and teachers abroad that gives information about overseas study, teaching, work, and travel by individuals.

Semester programs are typically limited to students enrolled in a sponsoring institution. On a similiar model some universities offer a full year programs for greater depth of study by American students both in their major field of study and in the culture or language of the host country. Other programs of international exchange are available where a particular university abroad and a American university exchange students with the host university paying some or all of the cost.

The American student abroad faces numerous difficulties; predeparture cross-cultural training might be helpful (Wilder, 1965). Most American students do not have adequate preparation in the language of the host country for serious academic work in the foreign university. Most American students do not have the proper prerequisites for the courses they will be taking or the historical perspective to assimilate the full potential of their experiences. Because students must give much of their preparation time to language study, they usually find it difficult to keep pace with host-country students. The students usually are not well acquainted with the methods of instruction and the university system abroad. Students expect course outlines, reading lists, regular exams, and structured instruction in the United States (although this has changed during recent years), whereas abroad they are more often expected to work independently in a less-structured environment. The American student is often unprepared for the examination system which in some foreign countries may relate less to the lectures and which are intended to evaluate extensive independent study on a given subject. There are many fewer counselors and advisory staff available in foreign universities to assist the students than they may be accustomed to back home.

American faculty members abroad have also increased in

number. Study travel is most frequent to Europe (57%), followed by the Far East (12%), Latin America (10%), Near and Middle East (5%), Africa (6%), Oceania (3%), and North America (1%). Their academic fields were concentrated in the humanities (31%), followed by social sciences (20%), physical and life sciences (17%), education (5%), engineering (5%), medical sciences (8%), and agriculture (7%). Twenty-six United States institutions reported having 50 or more faculty members abroad in the 1971–1972 academic year.

The problems of faculty abroad are in many ways similar to those of students in foreign countries. An early study by Gullahorn and Gullahorn (1960) on Fulbright professors overseas indicated that equal status relationships between persons from different cultures was a primary factor in establishing close interpersonal relationships and international training. The prerequisite skills for success as a Fulbright professor were identified by Goodwin (1964) and can be described as a four-stage process. In the first stage professors initiate activity of exploring the situation to discover how they might fulfill their valued goals. In the second stage they carry out a "probing activity" in a style that does not alienate significant others in the host country. The third stage involves learning about the rules and host country organization from the consequences of his own activities. The fourth stage requires the reorganization of activities on the basis of new understanding of the host country situation. One of the most valuable aspects of this exchange has been the establishment of ongoing professional relationships between host country colleagues following the international experience. The establishing of informal professional relationships is perhaps the most significant accomplishment of the program.

There are numerous opportunities for cross-cultural training both in preparing American faculty and students for their international experience and debriefing them upon their return home. The educational potential of such an experience goes far beyond a relaxing sabatical abroad or an extended vacation from the more familiar setting of an American university. An adequate training program should be sensitive to individual needs of participants as well as to the unique advantages or disadvantages of host country universities. A careful matching of resources could enhance this experience to the advantage of everyone concerned.

Mental Health Service Agencies

Cross-cultural training is useful to mental health service agencies for a number of reasons. First of all, the traditional systems of mental health services have a cultural bias favoring certain social classes over others, which is counterproductive to the equitable distribution of services. Second, other cultural groups have discovered indigenous modes of coping and treatment which not only work better for them but may be usefully applied to other cultural groups as well. Third, community mental health services are expensive when they fail, as measured by operating costs and by the useless expenditure of lives, and cross-cultural training might prevent some programs from failure. Fourth, the resources for cross-cultural training in mental health services are readily available throughout our plural society within the very populations supposed to benefit from those services.

The concepts of "health" and "normal" that guide the delivery of mental health services are universally shared by all persons from every culture and may betray the culturally encapsulated counselor to be a tool of his own dominant political, social, or economic values. Ethnocentric notions of adjustment tend to ignore inherent cultural values, allowing the encapsulated counselor to evade reality while maintaining a cocoon of internalized value presuppositions about what is "good" for the counselee. This tendency toward cultural isolation is accentuated by the inherent capacity of culture-bound and time-honored values to protect themselves against the tentativeness of new knowledge. The very data that define the task of counseling can take on another meaning in reinforcing modal stereotypes of cultural groups, separating counselors from the social reality of people from other cultures.

Systematic study of the interelationship between culture and personality has, until fairly recently, been limited to anthropologists literature is polarized into two opposing ways of looking at culture in relation to personality (Caudill and Lin, 1969). One position takes the view that there is a fixed description of mental health whose observation is obscured by cultural distortions and which requires the rigors of cross-cultural research to relate cultural behaviors to some universal definition of acceptable behavior. This position assumes that we know the meaning of health and well-adjusted happiness whatever the culture of origin. A contrasting position views cross-cultural differences as clues to divergent attitudes, values, and assumptions that differentiate one culture from another in a relativist framework. In the second alternative each sociocultural context defines its own norms of mental health. Anthropologists have tended to take a relativist position in classifying and categorizing psychological phenomena, identifying deviations as culturally uniques, allowing multiple notions of acceptable behaviors to coexist with one another in the cross-cultural situation, and examining each culture as a separate configuration. Psychologists, on the other hand, have tended to link social characteristics and psychological phenomena with a minimum of attention to intercultural maps of differential cultural values. Draguns (1973) claimed that only with the recent emergence of social psychiatry as a discipline have systematic observations been applied to the influence of social and cultural factors upon psychopathological systems.

Cultural difference affect the delivery of mental health services in a number of ways. Ethnic and class differences have produced a deficit hypothesis (explained but not defended by Cole and Bruner, 1972) which assumes that a poverty community is disorganized and that the disorganization presents itself in various forms of deficit. The implication is that minorities are somehow not only different in their cultural values but inferior in comparison with white, middle-class values. Havinghurst (1971) identified social class rather than ethnic factors as differentiating achievement, and Mayeske (1971) provides abundant evidence that there is no independent effect by ethnic-racial group membership on academic achievement. In an attempt to deal appropriately with cultural differences, Flaugher, Campbell and Pike (1969) concluded that closer attention must be given to the assumptions of predictive studies, recognizing that unperceived and uncontrolled combinations of influences on criterion measures may determine results as readily as the predictive measures being evaluated. Freeberg (1969) and Brislin, Lonner, and Thorndike (1973), for example, describes many of these unspecific biases in the use of tests. Psychologists have thus failed in the task of analyzing the source of cultural differences in a setting in which those same cultural groups are in competition for limited resources.

Reviewing the literature leaves the reader with a clear impression that psychological services in the mental health field need to become more sensitive to cultural differences. The criticism is not limited to members of radical groups, who, like Agel (1971), describe therapy today as a commodity and means of social control. Leaders in the field like C. H. Patterson (1972) are also not hesitant to point out the need for change in an activist mode:

> If there is anything that young people, the poor, and minority groups are telling us it is that they are fed up with our impersonal, inhuman society. They do not want more 'services,' automated and impersonal, even if they are delivered on a silver platter. They do, of course, want the material requirements to live a decent life, but as a right, not as a 'service' from a governmental or social agency. But more than this, they want respect, understanding and the opportunity to actualize their potentials, or to become self-actualizing persons. Psychologists, including counseling psychologists, have an obligation to work for a social, economic and political system which will provide everyone with more than the bare necessities of life, and with equality of opportunity.

Helpers who are most different from those they help, in race and social class, have the greatest difficulty effecting constructive changes, whereas helpers who are most similar in these respects have the greater facility for appropriate aid. (Carkhuff and Pierce, 1967). Mitchell goes so far as to say that most white counselors cannot be a part of the solution for a black client because they are so frequently part of the problem. Williams (1970) likewise asserts that the white mental health worker cannot successfully counsel the "black psyche." Ayres (1970) and Russel (1970) describe an implicit or sometimes explicit bias in the counseling process itself that is frequently perceived as demeaning, debilitating, patronizing, and dehumanizing.

In cross-cultural counseling (Pedersen et al, 1975), there is a great danger of mutual misunderstanding, less understanding of the other culture's unique problems, and a natural hostility that destroys rapport and greater negative transference toward the counselor. There is a danger of confusing a client's appropriate cultural response with neurotic transference. Ignorance of one another's culture contributes to resistance in opposing the goals of counseling. This resistance is usually accompanied by some feelings of hostility, threat, or unwillingness to allow the stranger access to a client's real feelings. Although some counselors underemphasize cultural differences, others overemphasize the differences, thereby depersonalizing clients from other cultures, which is equally dangerous.

Some of research has attempted to relate personal qualities of the counselor to cross-cultural effectiveness in counseling. We might expect counselors who are open-minded to have less difficulty than the more dogmatic counselor. Indeed, Kempt (1962) and Mezzano (1969) find that open-minded counselors to excell in supportive understanding and self-exploration usually associated with counseling effectiveness, whereas prejudice or factors related to prejudice were negatively associated with counseling effectiveness.

Cultural sensitivity relates to an awareness of indigenous resources within the other culture. Torrey (1970) gives an example of why urban Mexican-Americans fail to utilize modern mental health services, even when available. These systems are irrelevant because they are inaccessible, are inhibited by a language problem, are class bound, with the quality of treatment dependent on the individual's class, are culture bound and insensitive to the indigenous world view, are caste bound relating primarily to the ruling Anglo community, and because the indigenous alternatives are more popular. Each life style provides its own structures, rules, and mechanisms to cope with aggression and anxiety, and although they may differ from one another, they are able to promote and preserve mental health within that particular community.

There is increased attention to cross-cultural orientation in the mental health field, however. The National Drug Abuse Training Center organized a workshop on intercultural skills for drug abuse workers in 1969 to the extent that cultural difference affected both the problem of drug abuse and the process of treatment or education. George Washington University in Washington, D.C. is sponsoring a summer workshop on counseling minorities in 1975. Other workshops especially those dealing with problems of culture and mental health in a similar vein are receiving the encouragement of groups such as the American Personnel and Guidance Association through committees and divisions. Government agencies such as the National Institute of Mental Health have established a center for minority group mental health programs and are encouraging action research in response to criticism by black psychiatrists (Shapiro, 1974). The American Psychological Association sponsored a conference on patterns and levels of professional training at Vail, Colorado in July 1973. One resolution from that conference was that the offering of mental health services to persons of culturally diverse background by persons not competent to understand the culture of those groups should be regarded as unethical behavior. These are some of the indications that cross-cultural orientation and training is gaining importance in the mental health field.

Tourists

By 1976 international travelers are expected to be spending more than $40 billion per year abroad, including about $8 billion by American tourists. These figures do not include international fare payments to carriers. This expenditure, which is many times larger than our foreign aid program, will play a major role in determining the welfare of many smaller nations around the world, in adjusting the gold reserves, and in influencing the patterns of international trade for foreign consumer products. The money spent on travel goes far beyond the tourist dollar to include the whole travel industry, turning the same dollar over many times in the process. Waters (1966) claims that for every new dollar injected into the economy at least $2 of total purchases will be made, adjusting the dollar value of international travel by 1976 to an estimated $80 billion directly related to international tourism!

This figure is likely to increase, as incomes rise above the present average of $10,000 in the United States, as the larger proportion of Americans who have enjoyed higher education and are more motivated travel to foreign countries, as the World War II population explosion edges toward middle age and retirement with more time to travel, and as international imports familiarize people with foreign products. The International Union of Official Travel Organizations predicts an average annual rate increase in tourism of 12 percent on the basis of 15 years of data (Waters, 1966).

Tourism is a valuable industry to many countries that have geared their economies to depend on it. Income from tourism is being studied as a product like any other industry, with possibilities of depleting the "natural resources" of a country through cultural erosion by tourists. Tourism has sometimes increased the appreciation of native culture, bringing new appreciation and interest to the restoration and preservation of traditionalism. Ancient festivals are revived and old folklore is remembered.

The travel-oriented public is a surprisingly small segment of the population. There is a category of sophisticated travelers, "collectors of places," who have traveled abroad before and plan to go again later. Waters (1966) estimates that about 7 percent of the American public has traveled outside, with 6 percent of them limited to the Western hemisphere. There is also evidence to suggest that if the nontraveler can be persuaded to take his first foreign trip, chances are high that he will continue to take other trips. The incidence of repeat visitors has been high among tourists in almost every travel survey.

The resources of tourism are not evenly distributed

around the world. About 80 percent of the tourist receipts (perhaps a great deal more) go to developed nations, and only about 20 percent or less go the underdeveloped countries. There are many reasons for this phenomena. The predominance of developed countries as tourist targets is credited to four basic reasons. First, there is the health barrier, or the fear of getting sick in some of the more exotic countries, where the tourist assumes, rightly or wrongly, that he is more likely to get sick. Second, there is the facilities barrier, because many of the less-developed countries lack the travel, lodging, and other facilities that accompany the tourist industry that many travellers are unwilling to forego in their search for relaxation. Third, there is the information barrier, leading to more difficulty in finding out about the less-traveled countries in the world than about the tourist-oriented, developed areas. Fourth, there is the administrative barrier where many developing countries lack technicians trained in attracting and serving tourists who go there.

The problems of tourism have been the topic of an ongoing seminar at the East-West Center and a seminar on "Alternate Tourism Perspectives" sponsored by the Department of International Relations, Florida International University. The conference pointed out that the real beneficiaries of tourism as it now stands are more often multinational companies concentrated in the more affluent nations and that tourism has too frequently turned into another means of exploiting the resources of less affluent countries (Hiller, 1975). The question under discussion is: How can we minimize *both* the exploitation of host nationals by tourists and exploitation of tourists by host nationals?

The international tourist makes a considerable investment of time and money in a "commodity" of international experience with surprisingly little protection against that experience being less successful than hoped. Frequently, people assume that once one has arrived in a foreign country, the experience will automatically open new horizons of insight, glamour, and exotica. By comparison with other major purchases such as a car, new furniture, a house, or boat, tourists do considerably *less* to protect their investment. A tourist group or individual would benefit by preparing for such an international experience and by carefully evaluating what happened after returning to learn what has been gained from the experience.

Most travel agents have become less interested in educating the tourist once a ticket has been purchased, both because of the time and effort of cross-cultural training and because of the expertise required for such training. Numerous books such as the *Ugly American* have popularized the negative effect American tourists have had in foreign countries because of their naivete and lack of cultural sensitivity. Other countries such as Japan are now experiencing the same difficulty. As traveling individuals (and collectively as a nation being represented by those traveling individuals), we cannot afford to ignore cross-cultural training for tourists as an opportunity available to those requesting it.

Foreign Missions

American religious organizations have been sending personnel abroad for over 150 years and probably constitute the largest and oldest cross-cultural agency in our society. These efforts have resulted in establishing schools, colleges, and hospitals (in addition to the spread of Christianity) around the world. The effect of Christian missions established by Americans on foreign countries has been enormous. A 1954 report to the House of Representatives shows that Catholic, Protestant, and Jewish organizations were contributing over $120 million to technical-assistance programs abroad. By 1966 all nonprofit organizations, including religious organizations, were contributing close to $200 million, which at that time was more than the United States government was spending on technical assistance (Trail, 1966)!

The programs to prepare missionaries for foreign service are more varied than any other, ranging from some of the best to some of worst. A 1957 survey of Protestants who had left foreign service indicated that 83 percent lacked training in cultural orientation and 77 percent were without training in a foreign language (Trail, 1966). For missionaries, at least, there seems to be a positive correlation between the success of missionary training and effective retention in the field. The emphasis on missionary training up to World War II was mostly on language instruction, but after 1945 the training curricula was expanded to include development of particular attitudes and the understanding of overseas environments. The curricula typically include study of cultural, social, religious, and educational materials about the traditions, culture, society, and literature of the host country.

One of the leading schools for training, the Kennedy School of Missions in the Hartford Seminary, offered a two-semester course that included study of appropriate European languages and linguistics as an aid in learning local languages and dialects. A variety of new techniques in working with persons from other cultures, with an emphasis on literacy training, welfare, and public health work, is often structured in an anthropological framework.

The American Friends Service Committee have a training program that starts where people are and works on what they want. Success in the early and simpler projects builds confidence of the host culture nationals in the trainee-developer. The fundamentals of the Friends' approach represents the fundamentals for good training in any organization: (1) Involve those who are to be developed in the planning and assessing of needs. (2) Assist in the setting of priorities. Aim for an early success in one of the goals or priorities that is achievable, within reach of the group. (3) Start where you are, with the people you have and develop the capacity for self-help and self-improvement so that the trainer-developer becomes less and less necessary as those in the group learn skills.

Ziffer (1969) describes missionary preservice training on the basis of his experience as director of ACCUEIL FRATER-NEL Ecumenical Center for training of non-French missionaries and development workers assigned to work in French-speaking territories of Africa and Madagascar. He divides the observations into those relating to language study and to cultural preparation. In training missionaries he has identified danger signals indicating persons who are blocked in language learning. Poor ability to express one's own native language can relate to incoherent sentence structure, a tendency to abandon a sentence when only partly finished and switching to a new one, weak vocabulary, inability to articulate thoughts clearly and succinctly, extreme slowness in thinking and in expression, and poor reading ability. A second danger signal is if the trainee speaks in very strong regional dialects such as a southern drawl, midwestern twang, or pronounced slurring. A third signal is extreme shyness. Any of these signals suggests that the trainee will have greater difficulty in language training.

Because the missionary is usually selected before training, when these difficulties arise during the training process the church must decide whether to send the person anyway or, sacrificing the considerable investment already made, encourage the person to withdraw. The policy of training persons who are already selected rather than selecting from persons who are already partly trained contributes greatly to this dilemma whenever it arises. Ziffer (1969) recommended that missionary candidates would be better selected if given tests for their language potential, objective knowledge, cultural sensitivity, willingness to achieve, and a basic language orientation before arrival on the field. No rigid *a priori* time limits should be set on language study, with longer or shorter periods of training being appropriate to different candidates. The missionary should contribute financially to language school expenses, thereby increasing and testing his own motivation. Definite assignments should be made only after the candidate has successfully passed all necessary examinations.

Persons with more extensive training in human relations, such as someone from Stony Point Missionary Orientation Center in New York, lose their temper and sense of humor about as much as persons with no training at all when confronted with cultural ambiguity and conflict (Ziffer, 1969). He suggested that simulated training conditions do not usually result in real crises and permanent learning. Consequently, he recommended that the training could more effectively and probably more economically be carried out in the host country.

Bilingual Education Programs

American education, historically, has been a major component of the "melting pot" ideal once prominent in the United States approach to immigrants who spoke a language other than English. Non-English-speaking children entered school and were confronted with a teacher who spoke only English. If the children survived in the school system, there were ample rewards, such as acceptance as a valued member of American society and diplomas leading to high-paying jobs. But recently, surveys of school attenders and nonattenders has shown that the penalties of such an educational system are high. A survey was conducted in 1968 (reported in Kobrick, 1972), based on door-to-door interviews in a section of Boston in which large numbers of Puerto Ricans had settled. The results showed that of 350 Spanish-speaking, school-aged children, 65 percent had never registered in school. Similar depressing statistics emphasizing school drop-out rates have been provided for Spanish-speaking students in New York and Atlantic City (American Teacher, 1974). The severe problems of poor adaptation to a school system designed for monolingual, English-speaking children have also been analyzed for the case of American Indian children (Cazden, John, and Hymes, 1972).

One response to these problems involving various cultural groups and the American school system has been the establishment of bilingual education programs. Bilingual education refers to a school system in which children receive instruction in more than one language. In the United States, this means the language children speak at home (e.g., Spanish, Navajo, Chinese) and the language of the dominant, majority group in a society (English). The term "instruction in" is important. In a bilingual education system, children learn about different content areas (mathematics, social studies, science, language arts), in two languages—the languages are used as tools to study another topic. The situation most readers have experienced, the study of a language in school (e.g., German, French, Latin) but no *use* of the language to study some other topic area, is not an example of bilingual education. In bilingual education there are strong implications that the intrinsic value of the minority culture is being recognized, and that the majority society is responding to the need for making the educational system more responsive to the needs and desires of members of the minority culture (Lester, 1974).

Massachusetts was the first state to pass a comprehensive state bilingual education law. "The law declares that classes conducted exclusively in English are 'inadequate' for the education of children whose native tongue is another language and that bilingual education programs are necessary 'to ensure equal educational opportunity to every child' " (Kobrick, 1972, p. 54). More recently, the United States Supreme Court has reacted to a situation in San Francisco involving the status of Chinese-speaking students who do not speak English. Obviously, this ruling is a major precedent for other cultural groups seeking recognition in America's schools. The court ruled on January 21, 1974 in the Lau vs. Nichols case. The summary is as follows:

> The failure of the San Francisco school system to provide English-language instruction to approximately 1,800 students of Chinese ancestry who do not speak English denies them a meaningful opportunity to participate in the public educational program and thus violates section 601 of the Civil Rights Act of 1964, which bans discrimination based 'on the ground of race, color, or national origin', in 'any program or activity receiving federal financial assistance', and the implementing regulations of the Department of HEW.

Unfortunately, it is not clear from the ruling exactly what action is demanded: classes to teach reading in Chinese? separate classes to teach English to Chinese-speaking students? It is also unclear what the purpose of the program has to be. Some bilingual education programs are maintenance oriented, designed to keep certain languages (now said to be "dying out") alive. Other programs are transitional, designed to teach basic skills like reading in the mother tongue during the early elementary school years, but providing a transition to all-English instruction in later grades so as to prepare children for high school and post-high school education, which would presumably be in English. These are some of the issues with which bilingual education specialists are now wrestling.

The United States Office of Education has been quick to act on the growing demand for bilingual education. Nearly $60 million dollars were awarded for demonstration projects in 35 states for the 1974–1975 school year (American Teacher, 1974). The programs are funded by Title VII of the Elementary and Secondary Education Act, whose guidelines give ample room for the contributions of people involved in cross-cultural orientation programs. For instance, provisions are made for the training of teachers and teacher aides, and for preparing materials suitable to the needs of the children in the new bilingual classrooms. There are also provisions for involving parents, hence the need for orientation programs to acquaint the parents with the problems and possible outcomes of bilingual education programs. Longer-term programs to provide advanced training to key people have been established. Both authors of this book have been involved in projects carried out at the Culture Learning Institute, East-West Center, designed for people involved in materials development for and administration of bilingual education programs.

The general goals of the bilingual education movement are similar to the general goals of cross-cultural orientation programs: to make people aware of the important implications of cultural differences and to assure that people undergo a minimum of stress and experience a minimum number of negative consequences when they interact with members of cultural groups to which they do not belong. With bilingual education programs, the focus is on the school system comfortable to members of one (usually the majority) culture, but unfamiliar and possibly harmful to the members of other cultures. Good bilingual education programs are designed to reduce the unfamiliarity and unpleasantness.

Field Workers in the Social and Behavioral Sciences

It would be easy to presume that social and behavioral scientists would have a great deal of preparation before they depart to do field research in a culture other than their own. They have colleagues who have done field research, have excellent books to consult (e.g., Glazer, 1972), and if they are graduate students, have professors to instruct them in both formal courses and informal discussions. In addition, social and behavioral scientists should be most sensitive to the ways in which their behavior can adversely affect relationships in other cultures.

Such a presumption of adequate preparation and sensitivity is not well-founded, however. Often times, social and behavioral scientists have no preparation whatsoever in those areas we call the goals of cross-cultural training. This problem became clear to us during our joint attendance at a professional meeting to which many anthropologists[5] had come. Because we were preparing this book at the time and were collecting instructional techniques for cross-cultural training, we asked some very senior and prestigious anthropologists, "What methods do you use to prepare your graduate students for their first fieldwork experience in another culture?" Our question was met with a stare and finally a shrug. of the shoulders. Further probes revealed that these people did nothing special to prepare their students outside of helping them find a field site (itself a difficult problem, as we indicate below).

Perhaps the following anecdotes will help indicate a need for such special training. All these examples of cross-cultural misunderstanding involving social and behavioral scientists are either based on our direct contact with the people involved or have been related to us independently by at least two knowledgable people. First of all, it is becoming increasingly difficult for social and behavioral scientists to secure permission to enter a culture and do a study in it, or to find field sites for their graduate students. The leaders of various cultures are simply saying no to requests for permission to do research. The chief of an Iroquois Indian tribe in the United States has sent a letter to anthropology department chairmen, begging them not to ask for permission to undertake research.

[5]We do not want to give the impression that we are pointing at anthropology as the biggest offender. Anthropologists are simply more visible, because the discipline centers around fieldwork in other cultures.

"They are sick of being studied," a perceptive anthropologist told us after relating this story to us.

A second story comes out of a conversation, again during the preparation of this book. The first author was discussing cross-cultural training programs with an educator from Alaska. Among the ideas discussed was the establishment of a series of conferences that would allow Indian and Eskimo parents to discover what experiences their children encounter in school. The parents had not gone to the same type of schools, the current ones based on those in the mainland United States, and thus their children's experiences were completely foreign to them. The first author, in an attempt to establish more of a two-way street, suggested that the parents be allowed to examine or discuss the existing written materials on their Indian and Eskimo cultures and to suggest which might be used as instructional materials in the classroom. This would be a move toward preparing classroom materials that would help the children maintain their cultural identity. The children would then study both their first and their adopted culture in the school, importance being given to both through the selection of materials. The idea was applauded, but a cautionary note was sounded. "You are talking, of course, about the writings and publications of anthropologists, and 'anthropologist' is a dirty word. The quickest way to squelch a program is to say that anthropologists helped prepare it."

A third anecdote concerns the experiences of Wyn Sargent, an American freelance writer who visited West Irian in Indonesia, married the chief of a tribe there, refused to consummate the marriage, and eventually had to be removed by the Indonesian government. She took with her a number of native dresses and pieces of handicraft, which the chief wanted returned. Her experiences were written up widely in newspapers during early 1973. The point of the story is that when it is discussed, Sargent is referred to as an anthropologist, when in reality she has nothing to do with that profession. The feelings about anthropologists are so strong that there is apparantly a transfer of the feelings to nonanthropologists who do some kind of field work.

As a fourth anecdote, and to show that anthropologists are

not alone, we offer the following quote from Harry Klein, a resident of Tubuai, an island 50 miles south of Tahiti. It should be emphasized that the article is from the Sunday supplement magazine, *Parade,* seen by an estimated 30 million readers weekly.

> Klein doesn't think much of the other Americans he occasionally sees pass through Tubuai and the other islands. Missionaries irritate him; he thinks the code they preach is essentially alien to the Polynesians. College professors don't impress him either. An American came here some time ago to study the economy of Tubuai for a PhD thesis. Comments Klein sourly: 'Now he'll go home and write a bloody lot of junk. What for? Maybe it's good for him. Might even make him a big man, a professor. Then he can teach the same junk to other students. Here no one will ever read it or care about it. (Harrington, 1973, p. 22).

Finally, although we do not know of a lengthy anecdote about our own discipline, psychology (perhaps for reasons of self-esteem maintenance), we have been assured by field workers that psychologists in various cultures have been met not only with indifference and distrust but with downright hostility. One of us elaborated on these feelings elsewhere (Brislin, Bochner, and Lonner, 1975).

Why the negative feelings toward field workers? We have both directed programs involving participants from other cultures, and we have asked them this question. Our respondents have usually been too polite to answer right away, but after a little probing the answer, phrased in a variety of ways, centers around the "rip-off" issue. Put simply, people in the various cultures see the visiting field researcher come in, gather information, and leave, never making an effort to do anything for the culture. Often times, not even a reprint of the scholarly writeup is sent to those who helped with the research, never mind a popularization for a wider audience. Sometimes the research is seen as both inaccurate and harmful for the culture, serving no purpose but to advance the status of the researcher among his or her academic peers.

There are other reasons. Field researchers have often been insensitive to the nature of their funding sources, as shown by the famous Camelot affair (discussed by Horowitz, 1967; Glazer, 1972). In brief, people in the cultures under study see some research, because of its funding and the use to which findings will be put, as one more imposition of another country's viewpoint or values. Another reason is happily referred to among the more light-hearted field workers as "the CIA thing." This term refers to the question asked by the hosts of visiting researchers, usually late into the night and after five or six beers; "How much of your work is supported by the CIA?"

We hope that our treatment of field workers in the social and behavioral sciences has indicated that there is indeed a need for some cross-cultural orientation for this audience.

5

EVALUATION OF CROSS-CULTURAL ORIENTATION PROGRAMS

When the term *program evaluation* is used, it refers to the practice of determining whether a program (in this discussion, a cross-cultural training program) is achieving its goals and if so, whether it is worthwhile. Adding the word data makes the term *program evaluation data,* and this refers to empirical information gathered by people unassociated with the creation and development of a given program. We have found that very few people involved in cross-cultural training evaluate their programs. This is understandable because (1) evaluation is a specialty easily demanding as much preparation as for a career in cross-cultural training, and (2) it is very expensive to hire specialists who would come in to evaluate a program. However, we have witnessed a real distaste for evaluation going much further than points (1) and (2). We would like to take some time to point out the benefits of evaluation, starting with some observations.

At planning meetings for a cross-cultural training session, our experience has shown that most staff members will never bring up evaluation. That is, hardly anyone will ever bring up these issues:

1. Is there a better technique, as shown by the published literature, than the one we plan to use?

2. Will the people undergoing training learn anything, or will the staff members perform for a bored, inattentive audience? Will staff become bored or inattentive as result? Can we develop a method to see if people *have* learned anything?

3. Are we staff members planning on the basis of what we have always done, and thus what is comfortable, or are we planning on the basis of the facts available in the published literature?

4. How can we write up our evaluation in publishable form so that others involved in cross-cultural training (e.g., Peace Corps, business groups with overseas plants, VISTA) won't have to go through the same fumblings that we did?

5. Can we follow up program participants in the future? This would allow us to obtain feedback from people experiencing the problems for which we hopefully prepared them. It also forces us to think in terms of a long period of time instead of just the orientation period. And finally, feedback from participants who have received our training will be first-class input to future program.

6. In other words, do we have anything to show (other than letters and informal discussions with trainees, which are very biased) that what we are doing is any good, or whether we could be doing something better?

We are proponents of thorough evaluation, as we feel that it has abundant benefits (also see Campbell, 1969b). Evaluation allows the staff to assess what they are doing so that programs can be improved in the future. It also makes possible the adjustment of an ongoing program to assure a better effort, to correct mistakes, and to cover planning omissions. Published evaluations make a contribution to knowledge; others can read about what was done and what was successful or unsuccessful. It gives administrators information so that they can make knowledgeable decisions relevant to budget, for example, place, time, and staff. It makes many staff jobs more rewarding. This last point deserves further elaboration. We have observed that there is tremendous turnover in positions in which the staff members' main function is to interact with people who are the trainees in these programs. For instance, if the trainees are college students, the counselors and administrators in charge of student activities belong to the staff under discussion. There is little doubt that far more than 40 hours a week can be spent in direct contact with students, and thus staff self-growth is limited because there is little time for reading or individual research. The day-to-day routine is repeated, the job becomes boring, there is endless string of committee meetings, and for some reason such members receive the "drudgery jobs," a cycle that leads them to leave for a more rewarding challenge. If our recommendation became second nature to such staff members, they could constantly evaluate what they are doing, evolve a more satisfactory plan, and evaluate that. This is rewarding and exciting—to set goals (for instance, a good cross-cultural training program) and to see if they can be met. At times the staff member will discover a new technique unknown to the social sciences prior to his or her efforts, and thus will make a contribution to knowledge. If there were opportunities for such rewards in their activities, turnover among the type of staff under discussion would be diminished.

Our treatment of evaluation leads directly into the differential feelings held by staff members regarding human experimentation, which is often how evaluation is viewed.

Evaluation/Experimentation or NO

All forms of evaluation involve some form of data gathering, and these data have to be gathered from the trainees by the staff. Some staff members are uncomfortable about having trainees be part of an evaluation, and indeed a few trainees sometimes react negatively. Part of this view is the thought in many people's minds that an evaluation procedure is the same as participating in an experiment. The negative staff attitude is usually based on unfavorable feelings toward "manipulation," or the fact that they, as staff, are forcing people into an evaluative/experimental situation. Defensively, some staff members ask, "What's in it for the trainees themselves?" in an evaluation or an experiment.

Evaluation, as it is used here, includes participants' reports concerning what is good and what is bad about the experience that they have gone through. Evaluation is central to improvement of any program, for instance, college teaching. Professors at many colleges are evaluated by their students, and the poor ones (if they do not have tenure) either improve or are not allowed to teach again. Workers are evaluated periodically to determine whether pay raises or promotions will be forthcoming. Without evaluation, a system would be stagnant, never improving itself. An evaluation is different from an experiment, in the latter, people who have undergone different experiences are compared. For instance, one group might receive a certain type of training, a second group another type, and they are then compared to see if one group has learned more than the other.

Experimentation in cross-cultural training usually involves at least two evaluations (as we have used the term). For instance, some participants may receive training through program *A*, some through program *B*. Both programs are evaluated, and it is only when they are compared that there is "experimentation" as the term is most often used. If the results of both programs are compared to a control group of people who do not receive any training at all, this is a type of experimentation which methodology texts laud as desirable. As we discuss later under our "Designs for Evaluation," however, this type of control-group experiment is not always a practical alternative for the program administrator to consider seriously.

Experimentation is clearly an excellent road to knowledge because, when properly done, it can help an administrator make choices between different types of programs that might potentially be used. Consider the program *A* versus program *B* comparison mentioned above. If one of the programs is shown to be better by an evaluative procedure, then a person could argue that it should be retained for future use. Perhaps the evaluation will show that program *A* is better for helping participants to achieve a certain number of training goals, and program *B* for another, different set of goals. Obviously, such information will be extremely beneficial to a program administrator who can then schedule elements of *A* and *B* in future programs, depending on which goals are to be emphasized.

If an experimental design is chosen as part of an evaluation procedure, then the participants should be told about it to allow for a request for their informed consent and to give them the opportunity to drop out of the program (with as little discomfort to them as possible). We have found that experimentation in cross-cultural training is not hard to defend when properly introduced. It can be pointed out that large numbers of people have been helped because *others* have volunteered to be in experiments and that people *enjoy* being in experiments when it is explained what the purpose is and what is to be expected. For instance, the more interesting and readable textbooks that college students sometimes encounter are made that way because *other* students read early versions and made suggestions for improvement. It has been our experience and that of others (e.g., Aronson and Carlsmith, 1968) that people are happy and excited about making a contribution to knowledge. Altruistic motives can be tapped, because participants would be helping the *next group* of people who will be participating in the cross-cultural training. It is the experimenter's responsibility to catch the interest of others and to obtain cooperation from potential participants.

Having given some benefits of evaluation/experimentation and the feelings toward it that are held by different people, we would like to cover some aspects of evaluation that should lead to very useful information.

Qualities of a Good Evaluation: Independence

Evaluation data might include assessment of opinions and attitudes of the participants gathered through well-designed questionnaires and interview techniques, or the data might consist of a behavioral measure (e.g., number of hours volunteered for public-service activity) related to the goals of training. Such data is *a contrast to* informal feelings on the part of the program's creators and developers. Obviously, creators have a great deal of themselves invested in a program, and thus cannot be expected to judge their efforts objectively. It is far better to ask independent evaluators who are knowledgable about cross-cultural studies and who have reputations as good researchers to assess the program's effectiveness (or lack of same).

A recent television commercial may make this point clear. A distinguished looking gentleman says that "Some people still think that all aspirin are alike. All aspirin are *not* alike. *X* tested its aspirin against all other and found that for quality, *X* is superior." Our comment is that since the company tested its own aspirin, the results are suspect. Can you imagine the pressures on a company's chemist to find results in favor of his company's product? We are not saying that the chemist will cheat, but there are well-known baises in observing and recording (Rosenthal, 1966) in both the natural and social sciences that unwittingly favor the predispositions of the investigator. An independent evaluation team, with no investment in the product or program being evaluated, will produce more objective, trustworthy results. We suggest this informal test: after reading an account of a program being evaluated, the person who might use the information in the writeup could ask, "Is there anything here in the report that would suggest that the evaluator was under any pressure (e.g., job, future contract, or friendship with the program director) to come up with a certain set of results?" A yes answer on the part of several readers will force the evaluation report to be held as suspect.

Measures of Program Outcome

For the most part, cross-cultural training evaluation to date has depended on how much people *say they like or understand others,* rather than how much favorable behavior they actually engage in. This complete dependence on verbal methods is especially distressing because many studies (reviewed by Wicker, 1969), have pointed out that there is little or no relation between verbal attitudes and behavior, especially with regard to racial or ethnic issues. The classic study is that of La Piere (1934) who traveled across the country with a Chinese couple. They were politely served in every hotel and restaurant they patronized. After the trip La Piere wrote a letter to each hotel and restaurant manager asking them if they would serve Chinese people. The vast majority answered no. What happened, then, was that people *said* they would not serve Chinese, but actually did when the opportunity arose.

The La Piere study, and others examining the verbal attitude-behavior relation, have been analyzed in very sophisticated articles (e.g., Campbell, 1963; Wicker, 1969) and these are well worth reading. The much less sophisticated purpose of mentioning the La Piere study in this chapter is to emphasize that training programs that show positive attitude change do not at the same time indicate that more favorable behaviors toward host nationals are occurring. It should also be remembered that people can easily put themselves in a socially desirable light and say that they like people from other cultures (on a questionnaire or in an interview) when they really don't.

A related issue is the use of published, standarized scales. For instance, one goal of training might be to reduce trainees' rigid thinking about people different from themselves. There would be a temptation to use the Rokeach Dogmatism scale, since it purposedly measures high, medium, and low amounts of such rigid thinking. The problem in using the scale is that it was developed in the United States and was "purified" by studying responses from subjects in the United States. This means that many items were tried out in the early stages of the scale's development, but that some were discarded and some were retained because of low and high correlations, respectively, with each other and with a criterion. Thus the final scale takes the form it does because it was good at differentiating people in the United States in the ways that the developers intended. This means, then, that the scale cannot be properly used with people from other countries, because the scale was not developed in that country. Using one country's test in another is very similar to the mistake of trying to describe another culture's kinship system using American or "Yankee" terms. Some readers will recognize this problem as that of the emic-etic distinction (Berry, 1969). In addition, like most paper-and-pencil scales, a sophisticated person can answer the items to give the impression that he or she wishes, rather than to present true feelings.

Questionnaires will always be used in cross-cultural training, and we refer to their use often in this book. Even though our own preference is for more attention to and more research on behavioral measures to assess cross-cultural training, a recent (1973) effort of the Center for Research and Education (CRE)[6] deserves review. The CRE has put a great deal of effort into designing scales to measure the success of cross-cultural training programs, as judged by the participants in such programs. Although the specific focus of the CRE work was for the Peace Corps in Brazil, the content of the scales can be generalized for a wide variety of situations. The scales are based on statements about the program, and participants indicate whether a given statement describes the program. Scoring is somewhat more complex than the simple addition of a number for each statement (hence a sum total for all the statements), but once the scorer is accustomed to the CRE system, there are added advantages to the resulting scores, such as indications of participants' consistency of opinion toward a certain facet of the training.

The CRE has found it necessary to develop two types of scales. The first is the "Training Program Evaluation Scales," and it consists of the following nine components: (1) training staff expertise in applying Peace Corps training methodology, (2) training staff team performance, (3) training staff availability to trainees, (4) training program director availability and responsiveness, (5) experiential learning based on host country environments, (6) training staff responsiveness to trainee suggestions, (7) cross-cultural training method, (8) language training method, (9) coordinator of resources of individual needs. The second type of scale was developed because the researchers at CRE discovered that the nine scales already mentioned were not useful in assessing *specific* training activities, such as case studies and role plays. The resulting scale for

[6]The questionnaires are available in a technical report distributed by the Center: 2010 E. 17th Ave., Denver, Colorado, 80206. Title: "Improving the evaluation of Peace Corps training activities."

assessing training activities consisted of five components: (1) clarity of the objective, (2) skill of the trainer, (3) effectiveness of the method, (4) quality of materials, and (5) subjective estimate of learning achieved related to volunteer service. The CRE researchers were surprised to find that of the 14 scales which were developed, 6 dealt with aspects of the training staff, indicating the tremendous importance of the staff's quality and of the importance of the staff's performance during the actual program. We cover this issue in greater detail in Chapter five.

Our feeling is that there are now quite adequate scales to measure perceptions of program effectiveness, as viewed by the participants. More attention should now be given to developing behavioral measures to assess what participants actually *do* as a result of having been in a program.

Not a great deal has been written on behavioral evaluation. To begin the discussion, the reasons for the dependence on verbal measures should be discussed. Three explanations are suggested, based on our experience.

1. It is much easier, faster, and less expensive to measure verbal attitudes than to gather behavioral measures.

2. Program evaluators, when confronted with the challenge that their verbal measures are inadequate, fall into a defense pattern. They say, "You're not aware of the difficult field conditions under which data must be gathered."

3. So much verbal attitude data has been gathered in the past that researchers hardly ever think that it may be adequate. Researcher's apparently think that if everyone does it, it must be okay. Kiesler, Collins, and Miller (1969) makes a similar point, also criticizing the dependence on verbal methods to the exclusion of behavioral measures.

Training evaluation can be improved if methods like the following are used. For convenience only, assume Americans have been given training in another (host) country.

1. Instead of asking trained and untrained Americans if they like host nationals, ask the host nationals if they like Americans. This is the approach used by Spector (1969).

2. Gather data using "estimates" of behavior, for instance supervisor ratings (employed by O'Brien et al. 1970). These

ratings should *not* be supervisors' estimates of overall job effectiveness, but rather ratings of more specific behavior, such as
"How well does person get along with host nationals (as part
of his job)?" As Stewart et al. (1969) point out, the overall rating
may reflect many other job aspects than ability to interact
effectively with others.

3. When possible, gather behavioral data. This is the approach recommended here, and it will be dealt with in some
detail.

It is not possible to recommend a behavioral measure for
every situation. Rather, it is hoped that a spirit of inquiry can
be communicated through suggestions and anecdotes.

1. Perhaps money could be collected for some worthy
cause for the benefit of host nationals. The amount of money
donated, or the number of people contributing at all, should
reflect favorable or unfavorable attitudes. After hearing this
idea, one program administrator we know thought it worka-
ble, but urged that the collection not be for children. Americans have always liked children, and the effects of attitude
toward host nationals might not show up.

2. Analyze the number of requests to extend one's tour in
the foreign country. Some requests would be due to factors
other than favorable attitudes, but it would be valuable data,
nevertheless.

3. Analyze the number of friendships formed between
Americans and host nationals. Perhaps the number of home
visit exchanges could be used as the index.

4. Examine seating patterns in public places (e.g., restau-
rants). Determine if people from different cultural groups are
interacting or if the people are interacting only with their own
group. Brislin (1971) suggested a way of analyzing such data on
where people sit and later reviewed the literature on what
seating behavior can indicate about people's feelings toward
others (Brislin, 1974).

5. Determine how many Americans, on their own initiative, learn some host national language, volunteer for extra
duty that helps the hosts, or engage in other constructive incidents.

6. If one goal of training is to make Americans comfortable

in the presence of host nationals, arrange a party at which host nationals and trained and untrained Americans are present. The host nationals would not know which Americans had received training. After the party, ask the host nationals which Americans seemed most at ease and sensitive to issues in the host country. More trained than untrained Americans should be named.

In all cases, more than one measure should be gathered. This allows for replication of results using different methods, always a desirable research goal. The following examples will hopefully further convey the spirit of gathering behavioral measures.

1. Peace Corpsmen were assigned as teachers of English, one to each of several villages in the Philippines. The administrator estimated program effectiveness by sampling the English learned by the village children.

2. To test the effectiveness of a military training film recommending frequent bathing for personal cleanliness, researchers attempted to measure the amount of water used by trainees. The water meters of the barracks of trained and untrained groups were noted before and after the movies. This would have been an excellent test, but unfortunately, one faucet became stuck and emitted an unknown amount of water.

Designs for Evaluation

An excellent design for program evaluation, if there were no other concerns but obtaining the best possible evaluation data, would be as follows. The letter O refers to an observation, X to the cross-cultural training program, and R to the fact that groups would be assigned to receive training or no training at random (the shorthand is adapted from Campbell and Stanley, 1966).

$$R \text{ group 1: } X \ O$$
$$R \text{ group 2: } \quad O$$

The observations (Os) would be taken from both groups at the same time. They might be questionnaires and the sorts of behavioral measures already discussed. In practical terms, here is how the above design might be employed. On February 1, notices might be sent out that a cross-cultural training program is to be given. By February 3, sixty people indicate that they would like to take part in the program. At this point, the 60 people are assigned at random to the two groups, 30 people in each, the training and no-training groups.[7] This might be done with the help of a table of random numbers, or by putting the names of the 60 people in a box, mixing them up, and drawing them out.

The cross-cultural training program would then be held for the people in group one from February 5 to 8. The people in group 2 would go about their lives as usual during this period. On February 9 the observations would be taken of the people in both groups, and then the results compared. The prediction would be that the people in the cross-cultural training group would have changed in directions indicated by the content of the program.

There are minor problems with this elegant design, called minor because they have been effectively addressed in the literature many times (e.g., Campbell and Stanley, 1966; Crano and Brewer, 1972). For instance, perhaps people in group 1 will change, not because of the program's content, but because of the special attention they received above and beyond the content. This is called the *Hawthorne effect*, and one possible solution is to give members of group 2 special attention but no real training content. Technically, group two would then be a placebo control group. Another difficulty is that with this design, we do not know how individuals change in the training programs. To find out, we would have to take two observations of each group, as in this design, called a pretest-posttest design. This is another

R group 1: *O X O*

R group 2: *O   O*

strong design since we can compare the observations on spe-

[7]We assume readers are familiar with arguments that a group of people who did *not* express a desire to engage in the program could *not* be used as a control group because they would differ from those wanting training on so many factors other than the experience of training. Hence there must be random assignment of people *wanting* training, each of them with an equal chance to be actually *chosen* to take part in the training.

cific people both before the after the program. The minor problem here (again, covered in the references mentioned above) is that if the observations consist partly of questionnaires, it is sometimes easy for people to figure out the purpose of the evaluation. A participant might say to herself, "Here I am with a second questionnaire. It asks about thinking in international terms. Now I see why they asked similar questions on the first questionnaire and why this topic was discussed in the program" The person might answer the second questionnaire to please the program director. To give this problem a label, we might say that it involves figuring out the connection between the program and the observations.

The *real* problem for program directors in either of the two designs (much less frequently discussed in the evaluation literature) is that *people who wanted the experience of the cross-cultural training are not receiving it.*[8] That is, the people in the control group (whom we call group 2's) are not receiving the experience for which they expressed a desire. And regardless of abstract principles about the elegance of rigid evaluation, a program director feels strong obligations to people who want training, and rightly so. We hypothesize that one reason there is so little evaluation data on cross-cultural training programs is because program directors could not solve the dilemma between their desire to give people training and to not give it to others so that the effects of training could be evaluated.

What can be done? How can the conflicting demands of service to people and to program evaluation be handled? One of us is a heretic by even pointing out the problem as he studied with one of the world's top scholars on evaluation whose work was often referred to in previous paragraphs. In the writings of such scholars, there is a hesitancy to discuss the pressures facing program directors, perhaps because such people have never or have only infrequently directed programs from start to finish (e.g., planning, staffing, scheduling, and evaluation).

We certainly do not want to claim that we have the final

[8]The writings of Kelman (1968, 1972) have helped us in our thinking about this issue.

solutions. Here are just some suggestions. The first involves arrangement of schedules, often a problem for directors given limited staff and budget. This design might fit well with the director's needs to schedule programs, to evaluate them, and to give the program to all wanting it.

$$\begin{array}{ll} \textit{Time 1} & \textit{Time 2} \\ R \text{ group 1: } X\,O\,O \\ R \text{ group 2: } O\,X\,O \end{array}$$

Following with the same hypothetical time schedule, this new design has the same dates as the first one, with February 9 being the time of the first observation. Thus by comparing observations (to use some Washington, D.C.'ese) at this point in time, we can gain some insight into the effects of training on group 1, because group 2 has not (as yet) received any training and thus is a proper comparison group. Then group 2 can receive approximately the same program from February 11 to 14, and observations can be made for both groups on February 15. We would then have the following information:

1. We would have a delayed measure on group 1 to see if the effects of training are completely ephemeral, being observable only immediately after training, or if they are sustained for at least 5 or 6 days. Of course, we would want to observe again at a much later date to determine if there are true long-term changes.

2. We could determine the effects of training on group 2 —they should be similar to the effects on group 1. If not, perhaps it means that the training staff was not able to maintain its enthusiasm into the second program, a problem that the program director would then try to diagnose.

3. We would have information on individual change for members of group 2 because they received a pretest and a posttest. A more technical point is that we could examine the possibility or results, because of participants figuring out the connection between program and observations (mentioned above), by comparing the results for group 1 at time point 1 and for group 2 at time point 2.

4. Another important piece of information is that we would have the satisfaction of giving the cross-cultural training experience to everyone who wanted it.

Another design might be a possible choice when quite different types of cross-cultural training are to be used in the same program, and when all people wanting training are to receive it. For instance, lectures and role play interactions are quite different, and yet they might be used in the same program. This design would allow the program director to gain insight into how individuals benefit from each type of approach. Assume *a* is the part of training devoted to lectures, and *b* is the part devoted to role plays.

$$\text{Time 1} \qquad \text{Time 2}$$
$$R \text{ group 1: } Xa \; O \; Xb \; O$$
$$R \text{ group 1: } Xb \; O \; Xa \; O$$

By comparing the observations of groups 1 and 2 at time 1, the differential effects of training techniques *a* and *b* can be determined. Perhaps one will clearly be better on certain evaluative criteria, such as meeting specific training goals. By comparing results of the two groups at time 2, the effects of different orders can be determined. Perhaps giving technique *a* first followed by *b* will be shown to give better participant response than presenting *b* first and following it with *a*. Certainly, this would be valuable information for future programs.

In suggesting adaptations of designs for the needs of cross-cultural training, we do not want to downplay the tremendously helpful writings of evaluation specialists. The principles promulgated by them can be combined with the realities of the problems facing a program director. This can yield both good programs serving all who want them and good evaluation to improve future programs and to help other program directors needing information on what has worked well.

Other Designs

Oftentimes control groups are simply impossible. A program director might be asked to give training to one group at one time. In such cases a time-series design, well described by Campbell (1969b), can sometimes be employed. Behavioral events are gathered before and after training from the same people, at several points during each of several time periods.

Assume that the behavioral measure is the number of free-hours volunteered for programs aimed at helping host nationals. A time series, with training starting on July 20, might look like this:

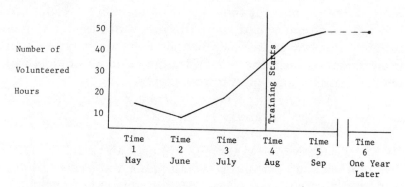

Figure 2
A Time Series Design for Program Evaluation

Of course, behavior would also be monitored long after training. Other explanations would also have to be considered, for example, Is there anything about the months of August and September that would encourage helpful behavior regardless of any training received? This example of different explanations for observations brings up an important concept. In a plausible rival hypothesis (PRH) exercise, originally formulated by Campbell (1969a), a researcher carefully lists *all* the reasons for his data in addition to his or her preferred interpretation. In cross-cultural research, plausible hypotheses often center around such methodological details as translation of scales, samples, interviewer biases, the specific questions used, and so forth. For instance, in college-level cross-cultural discussion groups, there are a large number of reasons why American students might have more input to the groups than foreign students, and in a PRH analysis these among others would be suggested in addition to the researcher's preferred reason: (1) shyness about using the English language, (2) a real cultural difference in assertiveness-submissiveness, (3) for males, chivalry in letting women speak in mixed-sex groups, (4) genuine feelings of inferiority, (5) boredom. Good research demands that data be gathered relevant to all plausible interpretations so that the researcher can answer every challenge to the study. In the ideal situation, a reader should *not* be able to suggest a reason for the findings that the researcher has not already thought through.

Another design might be used when (1) there is a very low program budget, (2) the program is to be continued in the future for other groups, and (3) the purpose of the evaluation is to determine program acceptance on the part of participants. The first program for group 1 can be evaluated by having the participants fill out a questionnaire like the following:

> Now that the cross-cultural seminar is over, we would like to have your final opinions. As always, be truthful and frank. Don't answer just to please the staff: Take into account the meetings, informal talks, chats with your friends, etc.
> The seminar was:
>   useful _ _ _ _ _ _ _ _ useless
>   bad _ _ _ _ _ _ _ _ good
>   helpful _ _ _ _ _ _ _ _ not helpful
>   interesting _ _ _ _ _ _ _ _ uninteresting
>   unstimulating _ _ _ _ _ _ _ _ stimulating
>   not helpful in allowing me to   helpful in allow-
> ing me
>   think about the future _ _ _ _ _ _ _ _ to think about
> the future
>   helpful in allowing me to   not helpful in allow-
> ing me
>   learn about myself _ _ _ _ _ _ _ _ to learn about my-
> self
> Do you have any other comments about the program? Please list as many as you like.

Similar questions could be asked about specific sessions within the program. The results from the evaluation would be used to refine the program for group 2 that would be given the training at a later date, and the process would continue in preparation for group 3, as in this diagram.

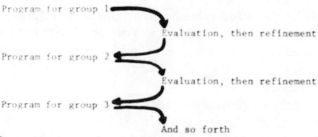

Figure 3
A Model for Evaluation and Refinement of Programs

The program, then, is constantly refined so as to obtain approval for participants. To use a concrete example, one of us (R.B.) administered a cross-cultural training program in which one of the sessions consisted of discussions on role theory, or the roles played by men and women in cross-cultural encounters. Participants, in their evaluations, complained that the terms were poorly defined and that there was not enough time devoted to an exposition of this topic. Because there were many other types of sessions that could be used, this "role theory" session was eliminated in the refinement for the next group scheduled to receive training. It might be noted that the session on role theory *seemed* to proceed satisfactorily, but the written evaluation (based on questions like those shown above) indicated much less satisfaction with this session than others within the program.

Note that the design would keep program staff "on its toes," for even if participants in, say, group 2 rated all aspects of the program as excellent, the staff would still have to work hard to have this high evaluation maintained for the program with group 3.

As always, if behavior measures could be used in addition to the questionnaires on participant acceptance, the evaluation would be much more robust.

To conclude this chapter on evaluation, assume that a businessman wants to sell a cross-cultural training program that cost $50,000 to a company. The company president asks, "How do you know your training is any good?" The businessman replies: "A group of trained people said that they liked host nationals while a group of untrained people said that they did not like host nationals. In addition, trained people were enthusiastic and some sent me letters telling me so." Will the company president invest money after hearing this evaluative data?

CHAPTER 6

PRACTICAL GUIDELINES IN SETTING UP A PROGRAM

Even though potential program directors may have an excellent grasp of the material in chapters one through four, a good training program will not be possible unless a number of practical arrangements can be made. We will cover these issues by relating our experiences with cross-cultural training in various parts of the world, forming a composite that does not represent a description of any one place, institution, or program. In effect, we hope to prepare others for the potential "culture shock" that may arise during their preparations for and the administration of a cross-cultural training program. We may or may not be successful, but *we* would certainly have had fewer problems in our own programs if we had been prepared for the issues we had to face. When covering specific examples, we will draw from our experiences with intercultural communications workshops, and with reorientation seminars at the East-West Center (both reviewed in Chapter three). A program planning checklist is included to show the sorts of activities that have to be scheduled. This chapter contains fewer references to other work simply because so few people have described the practical problems they have faced.

Staffing

The first and perhaps most central point about the practicalities of cross-cultural training is that when administrators ask for staff to contribute to the different training sessions, there is a tremendously divergent number of people who are likely to respond. There will be social scientists at the PhD or MS level who are much more oriented to the concepts of validity and careful evaluation of work than people not so trained. There will be personnel administrators (such as counselors at high schools or universities) who have tremendous pressures put on their time over and beyond that which would be spent on cross-cultural training. There will be moderate-to-high level administrators who do not want to offend anyone, especially those who control the organization's purse-strings. Especially important, there will be people who will soon be leaving their jobs. We have observed that the turnover of people in occupations involving some cross-cultural training administration is very high. Thus any one collection of staff members is likely to have a number of people who will be leaving their jobs within 3 months. Finally, there will be people who have no interest in cross-cultural training but who have been assigned the job by their superior. They would rather be doing something else.

Of relevance here is the fact that such staff members will have diverse views on how to best run a program. The most common disagreements are on structured programs versus unstructured—"just let it happen"—programs, and on experiential, participant-involving programs versus more passive approaches. At times, the program director will be able to hand-pick the staff, and like-minded people might be selected, or people holding various views might be selected. Either can be justified; like-minded people will have far fewer conflicts during planning, and divergent-minded people will have a wider variety of input.

Reviewing our own experiences, we have found that if there are more than five people involved in the planning for a program, there will be disagreements on how best to run it. The major division between people concerns the issue of having different sessions carefully planned versus having sessions develop on their own with no structure imposed or even suggested by the staff. During the planning for the first reorientation seminar at the East-West Center, a subgroup of the planning committee suggested various sessions that centered around issues that returning students have faced, as judged by letters from former students and the published literature (e.g., Cajoeles, 1959; Cleveland, Mangone, and Adams, 1960; Sehnert, 1973). Hence sessions were planned to focus on the issues of returning to family and friends, returning to the job and to colleagues, short-term and long-term adjustments, maintaining cross-cultural relations, and so forth (Brislin and Van Buren, 1974). Another, smaller group, on the other hand, recommended that no structure be attached to the seminar at all, saying, "Let the program develop as it will—the group of participants will provide the input, and no other structure is necessary than to bring the group together." Proponents of this approach sometimes charge those in favor of structure with paternalism, because participants are told what problems they will face. This borders on big brotherhood, the nonstructured proponents continue.

The majority of the planning committee voted for the structured sessions, and this is the approach we have maintained through five seminars. We certainly learned from the proponents of the nonstructured model, however, and incorporated some of their ideas into the seminar. For instance, we have been very careful not to *tell* participants about what problems they will have, but have always presented material that examines the range of possibilities people moving between cultures might encounter. In addition, we have added a session, designed anew for each seminar by the participants themselves, that has had little structure. Ratings show that the participants enjoy this one unstructured session in the context of the five or six others for which the staff has prepared.

We do not want to leave on an overly positive note, however, as this would be misleading. There were problems at the first seminar centering around grumblings from the minority staff group about the approach adopted. Participants overheard, and consequently some became less enthusiastic about the seminar. The recommendation, naturally, is for careful staff training prior to the seminar to avoid this problem, with the goal of achieving at least silent tolerance on the part of the dissident minority.

In addition, since the contrast between structured versus unstructured seminars has been mentioned, we must caution against one consequence of unstructured seminars that seem to us inevitable. If a group of participants is to develop the seminar and to provide all the input, then those participants with dominant personalities will monopolize the discussion. In groups of cross-cultural composition, this means the Americans; if there are members of other cultures representing both sexes, it usually means the males. As a result, the somewhat less forceful participants never receive a chance to give input or to ask questions. Part of a good program structure is to assure that staff members have been trained to gently guide the discussion to allow the "coming out" of people who would not otherwise participate.

Opposition to New Ideas

The first time a staff member in any organization suggests that a cross-cultural orientation program be held, there will be opposition simply because it is a new idea. Change is always difficult, and the establishment of a new program is a change in the normal routine to which people have become accustomed. We do not want to sound like fault finders, pointing fingers at some while extolling the virtues of others. Some resistance to change is normal in all people. The best way to handle potential opposition for this reason is for the staff member to seek the advice of all people who could have anything to do with the program. Such a procedure serves at least four functions.

1. It allows the staff member to pay a compliment to others because their advice is being sought.

2. It involves the others in the decision making right from the beginning stages of the planning.

3. It allows the staff member to receive genuinely good advice from colleagues.

4. It allows the staff member to obtain an idea of the people who might be asked to join the program staff for the seminar once it is ready to be run.

The *first* program that is held at any given institution is not likely to receive enthusiastic and total acceptance from the participants. Some reasons have already been suggested: interference with other activities, difficulties in reconciling divergent staff opinion on the best way to run the seminar, and difficulties in setting up the support services for the seminar. We feel it is important to recognize this point (again, a preparation for the future) so that staff members do not become overly discouraged when the first set of seminar ratings are gathered from the participants. Of course, recognition of this point should not be used as an excuse for a poorly prepared program. However, we feel that even with the best preparation possible, evaluation of an organization's first seminar will show factors that can be improved, and that these can be given attention in preparation for the second seminar. Since the "bugs" will be worked out, ratings from the second seminar should be higher. The process can continue: evaluate the second program carefully to improve the third, and so forth. It is important, however, to explain carefully to participants the nature of the evaluation being undertaken.

Unless well presented, participants will react negatively to the staff's evaluation efforts. At the East-West Center reorientation seminars, our major evaluation tools have been short forms which we ask participants to complete both before and after the seminar and after each specific session. At the first seminar, before explicit attention was given to the problem, the participants' reaction to the regular appearance of the evaluation forms was mixed, with a certain amount of feeling among some that they were the subjects of an experiment. This feeling was expressed on a number of the evaluation forms, and so we tried to improve matters for subsequent seminars. At the later seminars, before passing out a single form, we gave a careful explanation of the necessity for and the value of evaluation. We stressed not only that the members of this particular seminar might benefit, because there was time for the staff to read the forms during break periods to see if there were problems that can be given immediate attention, but also that, more importantly, future orientations would improve. We pointed out that the evaluation efforts of *previous* participants have been incorporated into the present seminar. Calling on such idealism, in the form of spending time now to help colleagues in the future, is not asking for a great sacrifice. Indeed, in most cases, idealism is a very strong element in the character of people who travel overseas for advanced study. Many times participants feel that they have not been called on to make positive suggestions often enough, and so they are happy to do so when given the opportunity.

Adapting Elements from Various Programs

We have observed that people who become involved in cross-cultural training rarely read or hear about another program and then use it themselves without modification. Rather, they take an idea from one program, another from a second program, and continue this procedure until they develop their own. This modification is due to at least two factors. The first is that program directors have to be comfortable with the techniques they finally use, and different techniques fit different personalities. Program directors, who work frequently with other people, learn a good deal about themselves by seeing how other people react to them. Hence the directors learn a good deal about their personalities, and they combine this knowledge with the nature of different cross-cultural training techniques. They learn about techniques that may be good for some people, but about which they might say of themselves, "I just can't be comfortable doing this." For instance, we have observed that certain people are excellent introductory speakers but are poor at leading group discussions or engaging in role-play encounters. Coupled with the need to match training techniques to the different personality traits of other staff members, the program director has to pick and choose from the elements of various programs, such as the ones we have reviewed. A second reason for the eclectic nature of putting together various training elements is that different programs are designed to satisfy certain goals, and the goals are rarely the same for any two programs.

For these two reasons we predict that this book will be used as a source for training elements rather than for complete programs. As an example of the modification process, we have complete information on how one program that we described previously has been adapted by a colleague. The program under discussion is the one we call "Reorientation Seminars." We refer to the earlier description (pages 103 to 112) as the original and to the revision as the adapted program. The original program was run over a 2-day period, but our colleague, Peter Adler, had only 2 day for his reorientation program meant to help foreign exchange students just before they were to go back to their home countries. He also felt that he should take the opportunity of the seminar period to encourage the students to re-evaluate the cross-cultural experience they had undergone during their overseas sojourn. Therefore, Adler started off his adapted program with the original sixth session on attribution and nonverbal behavior, because he felt that this would engage the interest of the participants and help assure enthusiasm throughout the program. His second session was a combination of the original first and third, return to family/friends, and return to job/colleagues. His third session was unique, being based on the group discussion method. It was begun by showing the *orientation* movie, explaining the benefits of the cross-cultural experience, that the students had seen at the beginning of their sojourn. The discussion then centered on which goals, such as developing intercultural friendships and an international outlook on problems, outlined in the movie had been actually realized.

Undoubtedly, the opportunity for a program director to add different elements will often increase his or her enthusiasm for the task. It is well known that participation in planning and administration leads to greater productivity, and in this case productivity means good programs.

A Person in Charge of Detail

The planning, administering, follow-up, and evaluation of the transportation, housing, food, and service is normally a job no one relishes and is often one that takes a back seat to the substantive portion of the program. This is unfortunate, as it can make or break participants favorable response to a program. As an example, for two different programs, one centered around an all-day picnic at a beach park and the other around a welcoming reception in a private home (both activities designed to afford opportunities for friendly social contacts of an informal nature) a great deal of resentment was generated when the majority of the participants felt that they had been slighted by being transported to the activity by bus when others (i.e., staff) went by car. At the third such event and thereafter there was at least one administrator riding on each bus; that problem has disappeared.

Many cross-cultural training programs are held at universities or retreat camps. Everyone knows that dormitory or cafeteria food is an easy target for criticism and a favorite topic in any "gripe" session by those who live with it. We forget, however, that people quickly learn various shortcuts to obtaining what they need to survive within the system, whether it be as elaborate as a small refrigerator in their room or just a good knowledge of where the machines are located that vend the snacks they desire at odd hours. Because some of the programs (with which we were associated) herein described were purposely set away from normal locations and food resources, much more critical scrutiny of, and comment about, the food available during sessions was immediately apparent in earlier programs (1972 in contrast to 1974). Evaluations of the different sessions began to break out with comments about the lack of taste in the food, its insufficient quantity, and its "Western" bias (i.e., there were not enough vegetarian type dishes.) During a later program the food caterers were asked to, and did, supply foodstuffs (in addition to their normal menu) at all three meals of a kind that would satisfy a vegetarian. Also at our request, they supplied the necessaries to offer hot and cold drinks, cookies, and fruit from 6 A.M. to midnight during the course of the camp. The dishes were simple but the supply plentiful at each of the regular meals. The kitchen crew (the same that had been criticized earlier) of that program was called out to be cheered and serenaded by the participants near the end of the stay.

Our recommendation, of course, is that there be a specifically designated person who will take the responsibility for all the mechanics of a program of this nature so that the details do not interfere with the carrying out of the important aspects of the program. Practical experience tells us this will not often happen. Thus this note of caution is directed to those who have overall responsibility for the program. Allow time for planning and carrying out these comparatively insignificant and annoying details, lest you find yourself in the position of man who, for want of a nail, loses the battle.

The Physical Setting

Many cross-cultural training programs are based on the participants' voluntary attendance, with the program director having no control at all over whether potential participants take part in a program. Exceptions occur when participants pay a fee to participate. Hence it would be expected that they would attend sessions regularly, and yet even in these cases participants can most often come and go as they like. Program directors find it difficult to impose penalties on nonattenders while at the same time talking about human relations and ideals of mutual understanding. One way of avoiding many of the problems leading to nonattendance is to give special attention to the place at which the program is to be held.

The physical setting of the program is very important. If we have learned anything for our experience, it is that the program must be held at a good distance away from the normal environment the participants encounter in their everyday routine. We prefer a camp or retreat at least 20 miles from the participants' home base. Without this removal from the normal environment, the situational pressures of invitations from nonparticipating friends, calls to the telephone or to the office for mundane matters, need to go to the drugstore for a tube of toothpaste, and competition from television take their toll on session attendance. Consequently, when the faithful see that attendance from session to session has decreased, their morale lowers. It is easy to argue that programs should be so good that they compete well with television and friends' tempting invitations to go elsewhere, but the realistic view is that much energy is needed just to run the program and that there is little left over to constantly worry about attendance. Our strong recommendation is that seminars be held away from a familiar environment that has a well-established schedule attached to it.

Seminars for Academic Credit

Eventually, the establishment of longer term cross-cultural orientation programs may be possible. An ideal arrangement for the study of cross-cultural experiences would be for universities to establish seminars that could be taken by people undergoing such experiences. These seminars could be offered to students during the semester prior to their return home. The longer period of time would allow coverage of material in a depth impossible to achieve in a 1- 2- or 3-day seminar. From reading about the experiences of others, however, it appears as if establishing seminars for credit is not an easy task. Sehnert (1973, p. 4) discussed "the difficulty he had encountered, even when his dean was involved in getting a seminar approved for credit."

Of course, procedures for introducing new courses for credit differ markedly from campus to campus, but at the six universities with whose procedures we are familiar, the following would be one way to *start.* A seminar could be offered through a given department (psychology, sociology, education, anthropology) under directed readings, directed research, or independent study credit—for some reason these are often numbered 499 or 599 (undergraduate/graduate credit) at many schools. All that is necessary, then, is that (1) such directed readings or individual research opportunities are listed in the college catalogue, (2) a professor, holding full teaching status or a joint affiliation with the department, is willing to lead the seminar, and (3) students are willing to take the seminar. The disadvantage of the procedure is that a seminar arranged in this way would often be an overload for the professor, who would first be expected to teach an established set of courses. For example, the professor might teach a full load of 12 hours of long-established courses, and the seminar would bring the total up to an overload level of 15 hours. This could be done by dedicated professors, but there is a limit to people's energy. In addition, this procedure does not give full status to cross-cultural seminars. Students can easily adopt the view that because the seminar is not listed as an established entity in the college catalogue, it should be considered as a second-class opportunity.

It would be desirable, then, to put cross-cultural seminars "on the books" so that they are included in the normal teaching load. We feel that the probability of obtaining approval from the various administrators who must review such new offerings will be high if the seminars are designed around solid, academic content. Our main purpose in this section is to suggest such content areas, with reference to sources that cover each in detail. Our feeling is that such courses *must* have solid content if there is to be widespread acceptance of them by academicians. A syllabi of existing courses in the general area of international communication is available in Prosser (1974).

To begin, a few background ideas relevant to establishing seminars for credit should be presented. We agree with Sehnert on the necessity for and the importance of a detailed study of cross-cultural experiences. It seems to us that if these ideas form a part of the suggested course content, the probability of administrative acceptance will be increased:

> Both pre-departure and re-entry could be considered subject matter areas of great importance and potential to international education, since in their study could be cultivated not only new insights into cultural diversification but also an awareness of the problem solving processes affecting social change and development in the respective cultures (Sehnert, 1973, p. iii).

Students who participate should be highly motivated to learn since they know that they would be applying the ideas from the seminar soon after returning home. We hope that the following light-hearted example will communicate what reaction we would like to see from participants in these seminars. Every once in a while a professor starts talking about a topic that causes a heretofore lethargic audience of students to perk up and pay attention. It is this sort of reaction in which we are interested and we are confident that re-entry-transition seminars for credit can be established that would sustain such a reaction across the entire period during which the course is run.

The key to such seminars would be that because the content is linked closely to the past and probable future experiences of the participants, there would be a great deal of interest and learning. The following list of content areas is certainly not complete, but rather reflects on our own interests and reading. Hopefully, others will add to the list.

1. The nature of the cross-cultural adjustment of the sojourner in another culture (e.g., Cleveland, Mangone, and Adams, 1960; Useem and Useem, 1968) is a good topic to begin a seminar, because the participants themselves have undoubtedly found the need for minor adjustments all during the time they have been in their new culture. From discussion of this type of adjustment, it is easy to move into studies of acculturation that are concerned with changes in society which demand change, sometimes stressful, on the part of its individual members (e.g., Spindler, 1968).

2. The range of orientation programs that have been designed to prepare members of one culture to interact effectively in another can be reviewed. Bochner (1973a) in a study of overseas sojourners who had returned to their homes in Pakistan, Thailand, or the Philippines, found that the overseas experience was likely to affect the duties to which the people were assigned as part of their jobs. Even when the job did not deal directly with international affairs, former sojourners were often given the additional task of being the international contact when there were visitors from another country. Likewise, they were often asked to give short orientations for people from abroad who were about to start work. The range of programs that might be reviewed includes orientations emphasizing lectures, group discussions, critical incidents, role playing,

video-taped self-confrontation (Brislin, 1972), experiential techniques (Trifonovitch, 1973), and so forth.

3. Individuals who undertake an overseas sojourn become more broad-minded and open as a result of their experience. One change is toward what Bochner (1973b) calls "mediating men," referring to people who are able to provide a link between cultures because they understand their own and the one in which they have lived. This concept and others related to individual change resulting from overseas study can be analyzed.

4. Educational programs that have been developed to maintain minority languages and cultures in countries where there is a dominant language and culture can be studied. Examples are some of the Pacific Island cultures (Ritchie, 1973), in which elders complain that there is so much emphasis placed on schooling in English that the children are losing their original language and culture, and consequently cannot communicate with their parents. Bilingual and bicultural education programs have been designed to put the native language and culture back into the school system (MacNamara, 1966; Lester, 1974). We would imagine that people who have had overseas experience would often be called on to advise on such programs.

5. Because seminars for credit extend over a much longer period of time than short-term orientations, it is possible that solutions to certain specific re-entry/transition problems can be examined. The one item that surprised us in Sehnert's (1973, p. i) report was that students in the short-term program about which he was reporting thought more time should be spent on solutions. At the East-West Center short-term programs we have never had this request, perhaps because in our introduction to the program we stress that all we can do is review issues. We do not know enough about each individual's home situation to suggest solutions—this has to come from the participants themselves. In the longer seminar, however, perhaps participants would like to examine potential solutions, because they would have time to do the proper reading about, and analysis of, a specific situation back in their home country. Such an examination could also include an analysis of the re-

ceiving institution back home, admittedly an awesome task because of the difficulty involved in obtaining the necessary information. A model for study could be that of Heisey (1974), who discussed the international educational program in Uppsala, Sweden, which gives explicit attention to the organizations that will receive the participants after they return home.

6. An interesting combination of academic discussions and classroom exercises might center around the participants need to be flexible and creative back home. There will usually not be the facilities (e.g., libraries, research laboratories, administrative support) that have been available during the participants' sojourn, and thus a more flexible "make-do" attitude is very useful. One of the major causes of unhappiness back home is the lack of support to which the sojourner has become accustomed; thus concentrated work on this topic should be very helpful. Discussion might center on the creativity literature (e.g., Stein, 1968), and the action component could include practice on the various exercises available that measure and encourage creativity and flexibility.

7. A theoretical concept that has proven important both in psychology and anthropology, the emic-etic distinction (Brislin, Lonner and Thorndike, 1973; Price-Williams, 1974) can be analyzed. The terms come from linguistics in which a phon*emic* analysis documents the sounds meaningful in any one language, whereas a phon*etic* analysis documents all sounds, whether or not they are used in a given language. The emic analysis, then, is for one system; an etic analysis is a theoretical attempt to incorporate many systems. As applied to cross-cultural interaction, the distinction can be studied through the culture assimilator technique (Fiedler, Mitchell, and Triandis, 1971). The culture assimilator is based on critical incidents involving people from two cultures, for instance contract workers from the United States and residents of Thailand, or White Australians and Aboriginal Australians. Approximately 100 incidents are written that describe interactions and possible areas of misunderstanding among people from two specific cultures. This specificity to the two cultures would then be an example of emic analysis, each culture (in this case, interaction among people from pairs of cultures) being studied

on its own terms. The emic analysis in the critical incidents often details customs in each of the two cultures that might cause misunderstanding. Some (not all) incidents, though, apply to interactions between members of other cultures, not just the two for which the incident was originally written. Certain of the incidents written for American-Thai interactions are applicable to American-Japanese interaction, such as misunderstanding due to public criticism of colleagues in meetings. Such incidents can then be presented as examples of etics, because they apply to a number of cultures, and because they can form the basis for theoretical generalization across cultures. With the knowledge gained from living in at least two cultures, participants should be especially good at understanding and using the emic-etic distinction.

There is a slight risk that a seminar based on content like that in our list could become a hodgepodge of seemingly unrelated ideas. We do not think this would happen if the major theme is stressed that the content chosen for the seminar centers around issues that are encountered, and that will be faced, by international sojourners. If the seminar seems like a hodgepodge, then the present, past, and future experiences of international sojourners have the same quality. But as more and more long-term seminars for credit are established, and lessons learned are communicated through workshops and publications, opportunities to point out the inter-relations among the component parts of a given seminar will increase. This will encourage a better organization for the seminars themselves and more guidelines for overseas sojourners (who participate in both short and long-term seminars) to structure their experiences.

Schedules Suitable for Different Programs

There is a range of schedules suitable for different cross-cultural orientation programs. In structure, these schedules would not differ from those describing any other program. The first part of the program deals with background, setting goals and objectives, clarification, and review of the schedule. The

second part allows the participants to know one another better, clarifies the workshop goals and concepts, establishes the
criteria for the workshop, and models the training design to be
used. The third part develops concepts, introduces the content
of the program, outlines the alternative viewpoints toward
that content material, and allows time to discuss the issues with
more emphasis on structured leadership. A fourth part might
apply aspects of the themes under study through exercises or
applications in some way, relating the theory of the topic to
practical application, with more emphasis on opportunities for
participants to lead and contribute. The fifth part would work
toward closure and some kind of conclusion, with emphasis on
evaluation, whether or not goals were achieved, and how the
workshop can make a difference in the participants' future. A
more specific range of objectives is essential to a successful
cross-cultural workshop that would allow leaders or participants to interject their own content material. There are advantages for the various types of workshop design that should be
considered in selecting the most appropriate format for a
cross-cultural orientation program.

1. The on-going once-a-week hour lecture is the more
ordinary classroom design. It allows the leader to work in
material over a longer period of time so that insights can be
tested out in daily or weekly activities of real life and the
implications of what is being learned can be reinforced. It
takes a lot of warm-up time at the beginning of each session,
and the weekly lecture lacks the intensity of some other designs, although it is best suited for the classroom situation or
any other tightly regularized schedule.

2. The half-day program can be used to introduce the
notion of cross-cultural orientation and to help participants
decide if they want a longer program. There is a danger that
in this short time participants might get a false impression of
the topic, or undervalue its importance relative to projects
given more time. This is particularly true in cross-cultural topics in which much of the material might be unfamiliar to participants, or in which resistance might be higher than toward
a less controversial topic. The goals need to be extremely modest.

3. The Friday-night-through-Sunday-noon residential workshop is very popular in providing a removed setting for both formal and informal exchange of ideas in a comfortable setting without normal distractions. If the participants are willing and able to spend a weekend together separated from the demands of their normal working environments, there are many benefits to a residential workshop.

4. The week-or-month-long out-of-town conference or institute is the most powerful alternative, although it requires considerable expense for travel. It brings like-minded colleagues together in a setting in which they can explore the theme or topic in considerable depth. The weakness is that most conferences or institutes have not resulted in a tangible product or result proportionate to their expense, even when they have provided a valuable experience on the more subjective level for all participants.

Modifications of these approaches are necessary with consideration being given to the financial resources available, the specific objectives of the group, the number of people attending, the level of knowledge among participants about the topic under discussion, the degree of intensity desired, the availability of an appropriate place to hold the workshop, the length of time available for a program, the appropriate degree of structure for those people and that topic, the degree of freedom by workshop planners to come up with their own ideas, and the overall purpose of training. The selection of participants is probably the most important single decision to be made and will determine what happens in a workshop more than any other factor, with heterogeneous groups being better for cross-cultural topics. At the same time, if the group composition is bicultural, discussion will be more specific than if the group is multicultural. A danger is that conferences on cross-cultural topics often are fuzzy in their coverage, with an almost infinite number of variables to deal with. Training directed toward a particular target population should involve persons from that population, both in the planning and certainly in the program leadership to ensure that the material covered is authentic. Where the facilities are available, immersion in the culture under discussion, in a foreign country or alternative culture, provides ideal conditions to talk about that particular culture.

Lynn Tyler (1975) at Brigham Young University, who has provided numerous specific and valuable materials on aspects of cross-cultural orientation programming, suggests a wide variety of design alternatives. As an example, he provides a planning checklist that might be valuable for persons actually organizing a cross-cultural orientation program.

A PLANNING CHECKLIST FOR CONFERENCES,
SEMINARS, AND SYMPOSIA

	Person(s) Responsible	Target Dates: Earliest	Latest
I. Preplanning Session(s):	⎯⎯	⎯⎯	⎯⎯
A. Objectives Established [Who? What? When? Where? *Why?* How?]	⎯⎯	⎯⎯	⎯⎯
B. Evaluation Criteria outlined [Expected Results, On-Going Concerns]	⎯⎯	⎯⎯	⎯⎯

II. Planning Session(s):

A. Program Outlined:
[Fund-able( ) Expedit-able( ) Use-able( ) Authoriz-able( )]

1. List of Potential Attendees prepared [Consider needs, practical applications, availability]	⎯⎯	⎯⎯	⎯⎯
2. Cooperating Organizations identified	⎯⎯	⎯⎯	⎯⎯
3. Topics to be treated defined (See I.A.,B.)	⎯⎯	⎯⎯	⎯⎯
4. Potential Speakers, Discussion Facilitators, etc. identified	⎯⎯	⎯⎯	⎯⎯

5. Tentative Budget   _____   _____   _____
   formulated [See all items above/below]

6. Public Relations   _____   _____   _____
   Program outlined [Advertising/Promotion]

7. Preliminary   _____   _____   _____
   Conference Description prepared

8. Preparation set for   _____   _____   _____
   Special Texts, Bibliographies, other materials

B. Dates tentatively   _____   _____   _____
   set: times and places

III. Expediting:

A. Budget approved   _____   _____   _____
   and fees established

B. Participants   _____   _____   _____
   contacted [Speakers, Facilitators]

C. Lodging and Food   _____   _____   _____
   Arrangements contracted

D. Special materials   _____   _____   _____
   ordered [Binders, name tags, references, etc.]
   [Evaluation Aids]

E. Press Releases   _____   _____   _____
   prepared and delivered

F. Brochures and   _____   _____   _____
   Registration information sent to potential attendees

G. Follow-up program   _____   _____   _____
   outlined for each item above.

IV. Interim Activities

A. Resource materials _____   _____   _____
   obtained [Aids for participants, texts, special materials]

B. Final personal _____   _____   _____
   contacts of participants, attendees, advertising
   pre-conference

C. Pre-conference _____   _____   _____
   Programs available [Speakers, Facilitators, Attendees
   listed—*Final check on facilities:* transportation,
   lodging, meals, equipment, room, materials]

V. Final Preparations:

A. Facilities: ( )Rooms ( ) _____   _____   _____
   Equipment (Audio-visual, recording, chalkboards,
   mikes, etc.)

B. Lodging and Meals _____   _____   _____

C. Special _____   _____   _____
   transportation

D. Public Relations _____   _____   _____
   (Greeters, problem-solvers and expediters in place)

E. Resource materials _____   _____   _____
   complete and assembled ( )for participants ( )for
   attendees

F. All speakers and _____   _____   _____
   facilitators present where/when/how they should be

VI. Program Conducted:

A. Evaluators using _____   _____   _____
   evaluation criteria (See I.B.)

B. Public Relations— _____   _____   _____
   departure details, final greetings arranged

C. Follow-up   _____   _____   _____
   suggestion sheets collected from participants, attendees

D. Copies of talks,   _____   _____   _____
   papers, notes, etc. for publication gathered
   immediately following sessions or definite
   arrangements committed

VII. Follow-up:

A. Evaluation (all items   _____   _____   _____
   above) [use copy of this check-list]

B. Gratitude   _____   _____   _____
   correspondence sent to all participants, attendees
   [Request critiques]

C. Printed proceedings   _____   _____   _____
   (if any) processed, sent as planned

D. Immediate planning   _____   _____   _____
   for next program (if to be held)

Conclusion

In this final chapter we have tried to cover a number of practical issues that can make or break a program, including staffing, preparing for possible opposition to new ideas, arranging for administrative details, and giving cross-cultural orientation programs a more solid footing by incorporating them, when possible, into college and university curricula. There is the danger that such coverage can serve only as an anticlimax to the coverage of the content and evaluation of these programs. Our point, however, is that without a grasp of the practical aspects of planning, administration, and potential opposition, knowledge of the more abstract aspects of program content will not be useful. Knowledge of both the content that has proved successful in other programs, and the practical aspects needing solutions are necessary if the goals of cross-cultural orientation programs are to be achieved.

REFERENCES

Adler, P. The translational experience: An alternative view of culture shock. *Journal of Humanistic Psychology,* 1975, *15* (3), in press.

Adler, P. Culture shock and the cross cultural learning experience. In D. Hoopes, Ed. *Readings in intercultural communications,* 2, University of Pittsburgh, 1972.

Agel, J. *The radical therapist.* New York: Ballantine Books, 1971.

Alevy, D. et. al. Rationale, research, and role relations in the Stirling Workshop. *Journal of Conflict Resolution,* 1974, *18,* 276–284.

Alther, Gary L. Human relations training and foreign students. National Association of Foreign Student Advisers, July, 1970.

American Teacher. Bilingual Education: its promises and problems. *American Teacher,* December, 1974, 16–18.

Amir, Y. Contact hypothesis in ethnic relations. *Psychological Bulletin,* 1969, *71,* 319–342.

Antler, L. Correlates of home and host country acquaintanceship among foreign medical residents in the United States. *Journal of Social Psychology,* 1970, *80,* 49–57.

Arnold, C. Culture shock and a Peace Corps field mental health program. *Community Mental Health Journal,* 1967, *3*(1), 53–60.

Aronson, E., and Carlsmith, J. Experimentation in social psychology. In G. Lindzey, and E. Aronson, Eds. *Handbook of social psychology,* Vol. 2, 2nd edition Reading, Mass.: Addison-Wesley, 1968, pp. 1–79.

Aronson, E. Busing and racial tension: the jigsaw route to learning and liking. *Psychology Today,* 1975, *8*(9), 43–50.

Asher, R. *In development of the emerging countries: an agenda for research.* Washington, D.C.: The Brookings Institute, 1962.

Ayres, G. The disadvantaged: an analysis of factors affecting the counselor relationship. Paper read at the Minnesota Personnel and Guidance Association, Mid-Winter Conference, Minneapolis, February, 1970.

Bailey, K., and Sowder, W. Audiotape and video tape self-confrontation in psychotherapy. *Psychological Bulletin,* 1970, *74,* 127–137.

Bafa-Bafa, A communication exercise. *Campus.* Pensacola, Florida: The Navy education and training monthly, February, 1974.

Bandura, A. *Principles of behavior modification.* New York: Holt, Rinehart and Winston, 1969.

Barna, L. Stumbling blocks in interpersonal intercultural communications. In D. Hoopes, Ed. *Readings in intercultural communications,* Vol. 2, University of Pittsburgh, 1972.

Barndt, D. The cross-cultural communications workshop. In D. Hoopes, Ed. *Readings on intercultural communications,* Vol. 2, University of Pittsburgh, 1972.

Barrett, G., and Bass, B. Comparative surveys of managerial attitudes and behavior. In J. Boddeyn, Ed. *Comparative management: teaching, training and research.* New York: Graduate School of Business Administration, New York University, 1970.

Barrett, G., and Bass, B. Cross-cultural issues in Industrial and Organization Psychology, (Management Research Center technical report, No. 45), University of Rochester: Graduate School of Management, 1972.

Bass, B. The American advisor abroad, (Management Research Center, Technical report 27), University of Rochester, August, 1969.

Bennett, E. Discussion, decision, commitment, and consensus in group decision. *Human Relations,* 1955, *8,* 251–274.

Bennett, J., and Passin, H., and McKnight, R. *In search of identity: The Japanese overseas scholar in America and Japan.* Minneapolis: University of Minnesota Press, 1958.

Bennington College. An inquiry into the effects of European student exchange. Bennington, Vermont, May, 1958.

Bermask, L., and Corsini, R. *Critical incidents in nursing.* Philadelphia: W. B. Saunders, 1973.

Berry, J. On cross-cultural comparability. *International Journal of Psychology,* 1969, *4,* 119–128.

Bochner, S. *The mediating man: cultural interchange and transnational education.* Honolulu, Hawaii: East-West Center, 1973 (a).

Bochner, S. The mediating man and cultural diversity. *Topics in Culture Learning,* 1973(b), *1,* 23–37.

Boehringer, G., Zeruolis, V., Bayley, J., and Boehringer, K. The destructive application of group techniques to a conflict. *Journal of Conflict Resolution,* 1974, *18,* 257–275.

Bolman, W. M. Cross cultural psychotherapy. *The American Journal of Psychiatry,* 1968, *124*(9). 1237–1244.

Braisted, P., Soedjatmoko, and Thompson, K. Reconstituting the human community. New Haven: A report of Colloquium III held at Bellagio, Italy, July 17–23, 1972.

Brein, M., and David, K. Intercultural communication and the adjustment of the sojourner. *Psychological Bulletin,* 1971, *76,* 215–230.

Brislin, R. The content and evaluation of cross-cultural training programs. Research paper P-671. Arlington: Institute for Defense Analyses, 1970.

Brislin, R. Interaction among members of nine ethnic groups and the belief-similarity hypothesis. *Journal of Social Psychology,* 1971, *85,* 171–179.

Brislin, R. An approach to cross-cultural training. *Culture and Language Learning Newsletter.* East-West Center, 1972.

Brislin, R. Methodological points in intercultural communication research. Paper presented at the meetings of the Society for Cross-Cultural Research, Philadelphia, February, 1973. In D. Hoopes, Ed. *Readings in intercultural communication.* Pittsburgh: Regional Council for International Education, 1973.

Brislin, R. Seating as a measure of behavior: you are where you sit. *Topics in Culture Learning,* 1974, *2,* 103–118.

Brislin, R., and Van Buren, H. A cross-cultural reorientation seminar held at the East-West Center. East-West Center, 1972.

Brislin, R., and Van Buren, H. Can they go home again? *International Educational and Cultural Exchange,* 1974, *9*(4), 19–24.

Brislin, R., Lonner, W., and Thorndike, R. *Cross-cultural research methods.* New York: John Wiley and Sons, Inc., 1973.

Brislin, R., Bochner, S., and Lonner, W., Eds. *Cross-cultural perspectives on learning.* Beverly Hills, California, and New York, New York: SAGE and Wiley/Halsted, 1975.

Bystrom, J., Casmir, F., Stewart, E., and Tyler, L. Intercultural communication development of strategies for closing the gap between the is and the ought-to-be. *The International and Intercultural Communication Annual,* 1974, *1*, 152–160.

Bystrom, J. Increasing intercultural communication: The PEACE-SAT experiment. *The International and Intercultural Communication Annual,* 1974, 1, 39–44.

Cajoeles, L. American-educated foreign student returns home. *Teachers College Record,* 1959, *60*, 191–197.

Campbell, D. Social attitudes and other acquired behavioral dispositions. In S. Koch, Ed. *Psychology: A study of a science.* Vol. 6. New York: McGraw Hill, 1963, 94–172.

Campbell, D. Perspective, artifact and control. In R. Rosenthal, and R. Rosnow, Eds. *Artifact in behavioral research.* New York: Academic Press, 1969(a), 351–382.

Campbell, D. Reforms as experiments. *American Psychologist,* 1969(b), *24* 409–429.

Campbell, D., and Stanley, J. *Experimental and quasi-experimental design for research.* Chicago: Rand-McNally, 1966.

Campbell, R. United States military training for cross-cultural interaction. NATO Conference on Special Training for Multilateral Forces. Brussels: July, 1969.

Carkhuff, R., and Pierce, R. Differential effects of therapist race and social class upon patient depth of self-exploration in the initial clinical interview. *Journal of Consulting Psychology,* 1967, *31*, 632–634.

Caudill, W., and Lin, T. Y. *Mental health research in Asia and the Pacific.* Honolulu: East-West Center Press, 1969.

Cazden, C., John, V., and Hymes, D., Eds. *Functions of language in the classroom.* New York: Teachers College Press, 1972.

Center for Research in Education. Improving the evaluation of Peace Corps training activities. Denver, Colorado: CRE, 1973.

Chaffee, C. *Problems in effective cross cultural interaction.* Columbus, Ohio: Battelle Memorial Institute, 1971.

Chemers, M. Cross-cultural training as a means for improving situational favorableness. University of Illinois, Group Effectiveness Research Laboratory, Technical Report 61 (68–6), August, 1968.

Chessler, M., and Don, B. Interracial and intergenerational conflict in secondary schools. The University of Michigan, Ann Arbor Educational Change Team Report, 1970.

Chorafas, D. N. Developing the international executive. (AMA Research Study, no. 83) American Management Association, Inc., 1967.

Clarke, C. The workshop—a statement of the intercultural communications association of Cornell University. In D. Hoopes, Ed. *Readings in intercultural communications,* Vol. 2, University of Pittsburgh, 1972.

Clarke, W. Overseasmanship spells diplomacy. *Naval Aviation News,* April, 1963, 12–13.

Cleveland, H., Mangone, G., and Adams, J. *The overseas Americans.* New York: McGraw-Hill, 1960.

Coch, L., and French, J. Overcoming resistance to change. *Human Relations,* 1948, *1,* 512–532.

Cole, M., and Bruner, J. Cultural differences and inferences about psychological process. *American Psychologist,* 1972, *26,* 867–876.

Conway, R. *The psychological effects of cross-cultural experience.* Belgium: Université Catholique de Louvain, 1969.

Cook, S. Motives in a conceptual analysis of attitude-related behavior. In W. Arnold, and D. Levine, Eds. *Nebraska symposium on motivation, 1969.* Lincoln: University of Nebraska Press, 1970, 179–236.

Cook, S. et al. Ethical standards for research with human subjects. *APA Monitor,* 1972, *3* (5), I–XIX.

Corsini, R., and Howard, D. *Critical incidents in teaching.* Englewood Cliffs: Prentice Hall, 1964.

Crano, W., and Brewer, M. *Principles of research in social psychology.* New York: McGraw-Hill, 1972.

Danielian, J. Live simulation of affect laden cultural cognitions. *Journal of Conflict Resolution*, 1967, 312–324.

Danielian, J., and Stewart, E. New perspective in training and assessment of overseas personnel. Alexandria, Virginia: HumRRO, Professional Paper 6–67, February, 1968.

David, E. You can take Rosenberg out of this country but. . . . *The Newport Navalog*, March 22, 1968, p. 4.

David, K. Effect of intercultural contact and international stance in attitude change toward host nationals. *Psychologia: An International Journal of Psychology*, 1972.

David, K. Intercultural adjustment and applications of reinforcement theory to problems of "culture shock." *Trends*, 1972, *4* (3), 1–64.

Decrow, R. *Cross cultural interaction skills: A digest of recent training literature.* ERIC Clearinghouse on Adult Education, 1969.

Devonshire, C. European workshops. Portola Valley, California: Center for cross cultural communications, 1974.

Devonshire, C. The facilitator development institute. Portola Valley, California: Center for cross cultural communications, 1975.

Dickerman, A. B., and Davis, R. G. Training managers in Latin America—A survey of company practices. *Personnel Journal*, 1966, *43*,(3), 57–61.

Dobyns, H., Doughty, P., and Holmberg, A. Peace Corps program impact in the Peruvian Andes. Cornell Peru Project, Department of Anthropology, Cornell University, (about) 1965.

Doob, L., Ed. *Resolving conflict in Africa.* New Haven: Yale University Press, 1970.

Doob, L. The impact of the Fermeda workshop on the conflicts in the horn of Africa. *International Journal of Group Tensions*, 1971, *1*, 91–101.

Doob, L. A Cyprus Workshop: an exercise in intervention methodology. *Journal of Social Psychology*, 1974, *94*, 161–178.

Doob, L. Unofficial intervention in destructive social conflicts. In R., Brislin, S. Bochner, and W. Lonner, Eds. *Cross-cultural perspectives on learning.* Beverly Hills, Calif., and New York: SAGE and Wiley/Halsted, 1975, pp. 131–153.

Doob, L., and Foltz, W. The Belfast Workshop: an application of group techniques to a destructive conflict. *Journal of Conflict Resolution*, 1973, *17*, 489–512.

Doob, L., and Foltz, W. The impact of workshop upon grass-roots leaders in Belfast. *Journal of Conflict Resolution*, 1974, *18*, 237–256.

Downs, J. Fables, fancies and failures in cross-cultural training. *Trends*, 1969, *2* (3) (Entire Issue).

Draguns, J. Investigations of psychopathology across cultures: Issues findings, directions. *Journal of Cross-Cultural Psychology*, 1973, *4*, 9–47.

Draguns, J., and Philips, L. *Cultures and psychopathology: The quest for a relationship.* Morristown, New Jersey: General Learning Press, 1972.

Duley, J. Implementing field experience education. *New Directions for Higher Education*, 1974, *2*(2).

Eachus, H. Self-confrontation for complex skill training-review and analysis. Air Force Systems Command, Wright-Patterson Air Force Base, AD 624062, September, 1965.

Eachus, H. Comparison of various approaches to training for culture contact. Air Force Systems Command, Wright-Patterson Air Force Base, March, 1966(a).

Eachus, H. Symposium on cross-cultural training, practice and feedback variables in the training of cross-cultural interaction skills. Paper presented at the Annual Convention of the American Psychological Association, N. Y., Sept., 1966(b).

Eachus, H. The analysis of culturally determined social behavior. In *Conference on Research in Cross-Cultural Interaction*, sponsored by ONR and Chaplain Corps Planning Group, 1968.

Eachus, H., and King, P. Acquisition and retention of cross-cultural interaction skills through self-confrontation. Air Force Systems Command, Wright-Patterson Air Force Base, AD 637719, May, 1966.

Egbert, L. et al. Reduction of postoperative pain by encouragement and instruction. *New England Journal of Medicine*, 1964, *270*, 825–827.

Eide, I. Students as links between cultures. New York: UNESCO, 1970.

Elms, A. Role playing, incentive, and dissonance. *Psychological Bulletin*, 1967, *68*, 132–148.

Elms, A. *Social psychology and social relevance.* Boston: Little, Brown, 1972.

Emma Willard task force on education. *Sexism in education.* Minneapolis: P. O. Box 14229, University Station, 1972.

Fiedler, F. Culture training and performance in multi-cultural situations. Brussels: NATO Conference on Special Training for Multi-lateral Forces, July, 1969.

Fiedler, F., Mitchell, T., and Triandis, H. The culture assimilator: an approach to cross-cultural training. *Journal of Applied Psychology,* 1971, *55,* 95–102.

Fieg, J., and Blair, J. *There is a difference.* Washington, D.C.: Meridian House International, 1975.

Filla, T., and Clarke, D. Human relations resource guide on in service programs. St. Paul, Minnesota, Department of Education, 1973.

Flanagan, J. The critical incident technique. *Psychological Bulletin,* 1954, *51,* 327–358.

Flaugher, R., Campbell, J., and Pike, L. Prediction of job performance for Negro and White medical technicians. Princeton: Educational Testing Service, 1969.

Foa, U., and Chemers, M. The significance of role behavior differentiation for cross-cultural interaction training. *International Journal of Psychology,* 1967, *2,* 45–57.

Foster, R. Examples of cross-cultural problems encountered by Americans working overseas: An instructor's handbook. HumRRO, 1965.

Foster, R. Dimensions of training for overseas assignment. Alexandria: Technical report 69–11, Human Resources Research Office, 1969.

Foster, R., and Danielian, J. An analysis of human relations training and its implications for overseas performance. George Washington University. HumRRO, August, 1966.

Foster, R., and O'nan, D. *Some resources for area training.* George Washington University: HumRRO 1967.

Freeberg, N. Assessment of disadvantaged adolescents. A different approach to research and evaluation measures. Princeton: Educational Testing Service, 1969.

Gael, S. Cross-cultural behavior as a function of attitude. *Dissertation Abstracts,* 1967, *27*(7-A), 2196.

Gezi, K. Factors associated with student adjustment in cross-cultural contact. *California Journal of Educational Research,* 1965, *16* (3), 129–136.

Giordano, J. *Ethnicity and mental health: research and recommendations*, National Project on Ethnic America, American Jewish Committee, New York, 1973.

Glazer, M. *The research adventure.* New York: Random House, 1972.

Glasser, W. *Brain drain and study abroad.* New York: UNITAR, 1975.

Goodenough, W. *Cooperation in change.* New York: Russell Sage, 1963.

Goodman, P. Hiring and training the hard core unemployed: A problem system definition. *Human Organization,* 1972, *28*(4), 259–269.

Goodwin, L. A study of the selection and adaptation of fifty American Professors under the Fulbright-Hays program. Bureau of Educational and Cultural Affairs, Department of State, Washington, 1964.

Grace, G., and Hofland, N. Multi-media training for cross-cultural interaction. System Development Corporation, 1967.

Graen, G. Instrumentality theory of work motivation: some experimental results and suggested modifications. *Journal of Applied Psychology,* monograph supplement, 1969, *53*(2), part 2, 1–25.

Greenblat, C. Gaming and simulation in the social sciences: a guide to the literature: *Simulation and Games,* 1972, *3,* 477–491.

Group for the Advancement of Psychiatry, Inc. *Working abroad: A discussion of psychological attitudes and adaptation in new situations,* 1966.

Guetzkow, H. *Simulation in international relations: developments for research and teaching.* Englewoods Cliffs, New Jersey: Prentice-Hall, 1963.

Gullahorn, J., and Gullahorn, J. The role of the academic man as a cross-cultural mediator. *American Sociological Review,* 1960, *25*(3), 414–417.

Guthrie, G. Preparing Americans for participation in another culture. Washington: paper presented at the conference, Peace Corps and Behavioral Sciences, 1963.

Guthrie, G. Conflicts of culture and the military advisor. Institute for Defense Analyses, Research paper # P-300, November, 1966.

Guthrie, G. Personal communication, November, 1969.

Guthrie, G. A behavioral analysis of culture learning. In R. Brislin, S. Bochner, and W. Lonner, Eds. *Cross-Cultural Perspectives on Learning.* New York: Wiley/Halsted, 1975, 95–115.

Guthrie, G., and Zektick, I. Predicting performance in the peace corps. *Journal of Social Psychology,* 1967, *71,* 11–21.

Guttman, M., and Haase, R. Generalization of micro-counseling skills from training period to actual counseling setting. *Counselor Education and Supervision,* 1972, *12*(2), 98–107.

Haines, D. Training for culture contact and interaction skills. Air Force Systems Command, Wright-Patterson Air Force Base, AD 611022, December, 1964.

Haines, D., and Eachus, H. A preliminary study of acquiring cross-cultural interaction skills through self-confrontation. Air Force Systems Command, Wright-Patterson Air Force Base, AD 624120, September, 1965.

Hall, E. *The silent language.* New York: Doubleday, 1959.

Hall, E. *The hidden dimension.* Garden City: Doubleday, 1966.

Harms, L. Beyond tolerance: World communication technology and the local cultural structures of man. In F. Casmir, Ed. *International and Intercultural Communication Annual,* 1974, *1,* 102–110.

Harrington, R. One man's special island. *Parade,* January 7, 1973, 21–22.

Harris, J. A science of the South Pacific: analysis of the character structure of the Peace Corps Volunteer. *American Psychologist,* 1973, *28,* 232–247.

Harris, J. The identification of cross-cultural talent: the empirical approach of the Peace Corps. *Topics in Culture Learning,* 1975, *3,* 66–78.

Haigh, G. Field training in human relations for the peace corps. *Journal of Social Psychology,* 1966, *68,* 3–13.

Harrison, R., and Hopkins, R. The design of cross-cultural training: an alternative to the university model. *The Journal of Applied Behavioral Science,* 1967, *3,* 431–460.

Havinghurst, R. Social class actors in coping style and competance, (mimeo), University of Chicago, Committee on Human Development, 1971.

Health, Education and Welfare. *American students and teachers abroad: Sources of information about overseas study, teach-*

ing, work and travel. Washington, D.C.: Government Printing Office, 1972.

Heisey, R. A Swedish approach to international communication. *Topics in Culture Learning,* 1974, *2,* 41–49.

Heiss, J., and Nash, D. The stranger in laboratory culture revisited. *Human Organization,* 1967, *26,* 47–51.

Herman, S., and Schild, E. The stranger group in a cross-cultural situation. *Sociometry,* 1961, *24,* 165–176.

Hiller, H. Guidelines for new tourism. Florida International University, Department of International Relations, 1975.

Himsel, R. *Life skills coaching manual.* Prince Albert, Saskatchewan: Saskatchewan Newstart, Inc., 1972.

Hitchin, D. International business education, the executive's viewpoint, a report on a survey of needs. *Training and Development Journal,* February, 1968, *22*(2), 36–43.

Hodgson, F. Cross-cultural conflict: an illustration of the implications for American business management overseas. Ann Arbor, Michigan: University Microfilms, 1961.

Hoehn, A. J. The design of cross cultural training for military advisers. George Washington University: Human Resources Research Office, 1966.

Hoehn, A. The need for innovative approaches for training in intercultural interaction. Alexander, Virginia: HumRRO, March, 1968, 9–68.

Hoopes, D. Editorial. *Communique,* January-March, 1975, *5,* 3–4.

Howell, W. Can intercultural communication be taught in a classroom? In M. Prosser, Ed. *Syllabi in intercultural communication,* pp. 1–14. Charlottesville, Virginia: University of Virginia, 1974.

Horowitz, I., Ed. *The rise and fall of Project Camelot.* Cambridge: MIT Press, 1967.

Hull, F. Changes in world-mindedness after a cross-cultural sensitivity group experience. *Journal of Applied Behavioral Science,* 1972, *8*(1), 115–121.

Humphrey, R. Fight the cold war: A handbook for overseas orientation officers. Washington, D.C.: American Institutes for Research, August, 1964.

Humphrey, R. Fight the cold war (Korean supplement). Washington, D.C.: American Institutes for Research, 1968.

Ingram, L. Some contrasts between sensitivity training groups and the intercultural communications workshop. University of Washington, 1975.

Institute of International Education. *Open doors, 1975.* New York: Institute of International Education, 1975.

Ivancevich, J. Perceived need satisfactions of domestic versus overseas managers. *Journal of Applied Psychology,* 1969, *53,* 274–278.

Ivancevich, J. Predeparture training for overseas: a study of American manager training for overseas transfer. *Training Development Journal,* 1969, *23*(1), 36–40.

Ivey, A. E. *Microcounseling: innovations in interviewing training.* Springfield, Illinois: Charles C. Thomas, 1971.

Ivey, A., and Gluckstern, N. *Basic attending skills.* Amherst, Massachusetts: University of Massachusetts, 1974.

Janis, I. *Psychological stress.* New York: Wiley, 1958.

Janis, I., and Mann, L. Effectiveness of emotional role playing in modifying smoking habits and attitudes. *Journal of Experimental Research in Personality,* 1965, *1,* 48–90.

Johnson, M., and Carter, G. Training needs of Americans working abroad. *Social Change,* 1972, *2*(1), 1–3.

Jones, E., Kanhouse, D., Kelley, H., Nisbett, R., Valins, S., and Weiner, B. *Attribution: Perceiving the causes of behavior.* Morristown, N. J.: General Learning Press, 1972.

Jordon, N. An interesting incident at the CIRADS just held. Institute for Defense Analyses, Internal Note N-354, June, 1966.

Kagan, N. *Basic helping relationships.* East Lansing, Michigan: Michigan State University, 1969.

Kelman, H. *A time to speak.* San Francisco: Jossey-Bass, 1968.

Kelman, J. The rights of the subject in social research: An analysis in terms of relative power and legitimacy. *American Psychologist,* 1972, *27,* 989–1016.

Kempt, C. Influence of dogmatism on the training of counselors. *Journal of Counseling Psychology,* 1962, *9,* 155–157.

Kerrick, J., Clark, V., and Rice, D. Lecture versus participation in the health training of Peace Corp volunteers. *Journal of Educational Psychology,* 1967, *58*(5), 259–265.

Kiesler, C., Collins, B., and Miller, N. *Attitude change: A critical analysis of theoretical approaches.* New York: Wiley, 1969.

King, P. A summary of research in training for advisory roles in other cultures by the behavioral sciences laboratory. Air Force Systems Command, Wright-Patterson Air Force Base, AD 648517, September, 1966.

King, P. Cross-cultural interaction skill training-a field test of the self-confrontation technique. Air Force Systems Command, Wright-Patterson Air Force Base, December, 1967(a).

King, P. Research in training for advisory roles in other cultures. *Research and Technology Briefs,* (USAF), 1967(b), *5*(2), 1–6.

Klein, M., and Alexander, A., Tseng, K. H., Miller, M., Yeh, E. K., and Chu, H. M. Foreign students in a big university: Subculture within a subculture. (Mimeo), 1971.

Kleitsch, R. The active case study. (Unpublished), 1971.

Kobrick, J. The compelling case for bilingual education. *Saturday Review,* April 29, 1972, 54–58.

Kraemer, A. The development of cultural self-awareness: Design of a program of instruction. HumRRO, Professional Paper, August, 1969, 27–29.

Kraemer, A. A cultural self-awareness approach to improving intercultural communication skills. Washington, D.C.: HumRRO, April, 1973.

Kraemer, A., and Stewart, E. Cross-cultural problems of U.S. Army personnel in Laos and their implications for area training. George Washington University, HumRRO, 1964.

LaPiere, R. T. Attitudes vs. actions. *Social Forces,* 1934, *13,* 230–237.

Lee, J. A cultural analysis in overseas operations. *Harvard Business Review,* March–April, 1966.

Lester, M. Bilingual education in the United States, the Pacific, and Southeast Asia. *Topics in Culture Learning,* 1974, *2,* 137–146.

Lewin, K. Group decision and social change. In T. Newcomb, and E. Hartley, Eds. *Readings in Social Psychology.* New York: Holt, Rinehart, and Winston, 1947.

Loring, R., and Wells, T. Breakthrough: women into management. New York: Van Nostrand Rinehold, 1972.

Loubert, J. The trans-cultural research and training institute (TCI). Human Sciences Research, Inc., Publication No. HSR-RR-67/7/Cs, April, 1967.

Lysgaard, S. Adjustment in a foreign society: Norwegian Fulbright grantees visiting the United States. *International Social Sciences Bulletin,* 1955, *7,* 45–51.

Macnamara, J. *Bilingualism and primary education: a study of the Irish experience.* Edinburgh: Edinburgh University Press, 1966.

Mann, L., and Janis, I. A follow-up study on the long-term effects of emotional role playing. *Journal of Personality and Social Psychology,* 1968, *8,* 339–342.

Mapes, G. An outgoing civilian tells outgoing sailors safe ways to have fun. *The Wall Street Journal,* August 7, 1967, *170* (25).

Maruyama, M. Monopolarization, family and individuality. *Psychiatry Quarterly,* 1966, *40*(1), 133–149.

Maruyama, M. Epistomology of social science research. (Mimeo), 1970.

Mayeske, G. W. On the explanation of racial-ethnic group differences in achievement test scores. U. S. Office of Education, Washington, D.C., 1971.

McGonigal, R. For want of an attitude . . . Quantico, Virginia: Education Center Marine Corps Development and Education Command, 1968.

Mezzano, J. A note on dogmatism and counselor effectiveness. *Counselor Education and Supervision,* 1969, *9*(1), 64–65.

Miner, H. Body ritual among the Nacirema. *American Anthropologist,* 1956, *58,* 503–507.

Mitchell, T., and Biglan, A. Instrumentality theories: current uses in psychology. *Psychological Bulletin,* 1971, *76,* 432–454.

Mitchell, T., and Foa, U. An examination of the effects of cultural training on the interaction of heterocultural task groups. University of Illinois, Group Effectiveness Research Laboratory, Technical Report 29, November, 1968.

Moran, R. Intercultural communication workshops: going where? Paper presented at the meetings of the Society for Cross-Cultural Research, Philadelphia, February, 1973.

Moran, R., Mestenhauser, J., and Pedersen, P. Dress rehearsal for a cross-cultural experience. *International Educational and Cultural Exchange,* Summer, 1974.

Nayer, E., Touzard, H., and Summers, D. Training tasks and mediator orientation in heteronegotiation. *Human Relations,* 1968, *2*(3), 283–294.

Newman, W. The personal response project-a communications perspective. In *Conference on Research in Cross-Cultural In-*

teraction, sponsored by ONR and Chaplain Corps Planning Group, 1968, 1–13.

Nylen, D., and Mitchel, J. *A handbook of staff development and human relations training.* Washington, D.C.: NTL Institute for Applied Behavioral Sciences, 1967.

Oberg, K. Culture shock and the problem of adjustment to new cultural environments. Washington, D.C.: Department of State, Foreign Service Institute, 1958.

O'Brien, G., Fiedler, F., and Hewlett, T. The effects of programmed culture training upon the performance of volunteer medical teams in Central America. Seattle: Organizational Research, University of Washington, 1970.

Padilla, E., Boxley, R., and Wagner, N. The desegregation of clinical psychology training. Paper presented at the meeting of the American Psychological Association, Honolulu, 1972.

Patterson, C. H. Presidents message: Counseling psychology in the 1970's. *The Counseling Psychologist,* 1972, *3*(2), 4.

Pedersen, P. A cross-cultural coalition training model for educating mental health professionals to function in multicultural populations. Paper presented at the IXth International Congress of Ethnological and Anthropological Sciences, Chicago, September, 1973.

Pedersen, P. Critical incidents in cross cultural communications: A manual. Minneapolis: International Student Advisor's Office, 1974.

Pedersen, P. A bilingual alternative for higher education. *Culture and Language Learning Newsletter,* 1975(a), East-West Center, *3*(3).

Pedersen, P. Personal problem solving resources used by University of Minnesota foreign students. *Topics in Culture Learning,* 1975(b), *3,* 55–65.

Pedersen, P., Lonner, W., and Draguns, J., Eds. *Counseling Across Cultures.* Honolulu, Hawaii: University Press of Hawaii, 1975.

Price-Williams, D. Psychological experiment and anthropology: the problem of categories. *Ethos,* 1974, *2,* 95–114.

Prosser, M. Syllabi in intercultural communication: 1974. Charlottesville, Virginia: Speech and Communication Department, University of Virginia, December, 1974.

Reivich, R., and Geertsma, R. Observational media and psychotherapy training. *Journal of Nervous and Mental Disorders,* 1969, *148,* 310–327.

Resnick, J., and Schwartz, T. Ethical standards as an independent variable in psychological research. *American Psychologist,* 1973, *28,* 134–139.

Rhinesmith, S. Training for cross-cultural operations. *Training and Development Journal,* 1970, *24,* 20–23.

Ritchie, J. Teaching the Social Sciences: innovation in small systems. *Topics in Culture Learning,* 1973, *1,* 48–60.

Rosenberg, D. Area orientation/overseasmanship training fact sheet. Unpublished paper, 1970.

Rosenthal, R. *Experimenter effects in behavior research.* New York: Appleton-Century-Crofts, 1966.

Roth, R. Cross-cultural interaction and some understandings leading to training emphasis. NATO Conference on Special Training for Multilateral Forces, Brussels, July, 1969.

Russel, R. D. Black perceptions of guidance. *The Personnel and Guidance Journal,* 1970, *48,* 721–729.

Sehnert, F. A report of the second SIU-MOHONK Trust follow-up re-entry consultation. Office of International Education, Southern Illinois University, 1973.

Selby, H., and Woods, C. Foreign students at a high pressure university. Stanford University: Institute for the study of human problems, 1962.

Selltiz, C., Christ, R., Havel, J., and Cook, S. *Attitudes and social relations of foreign students in the United States.* Minneapolis: University of Minnesota Press, 1963.

Semas, P. Foreign students: more coming. *The Chronicle of Higher Education,* March 24, 1975, *10*(5), 6.

Sewell, W., and Davidson, O. *Scandinavian students on an American Campus.* Minneapolis: University of Minnesota Press, 1961.

Shapiro, R. Racism and community mental health. Paper presented at the East Arkansas Regional Mental Health Center, Helena, Arkansas, October 22, 1974.

Sherif, M. Superordinate goals in the reduction of intergroup conflicts. *American Journal of Sociology,* 1958, *63,* 349–356.

Sherif, M. *Group conflict and cooperation: their social psychology.* London: Routledge and Kegan Paul, 1967.

Shubik, M. *Game theory and related approaches to social behavior.* New York: John Wiley and Sons, 1964.

Silverthorne, C., and Goldberg, R. American-foreign student cross cultural human relations laboratory: A report. In D. Hoopes, Ed. *Readings in intercultural communications,* Vol. 2, 1972, University of Pittsburgh.

Simon, S., Howe, L., and Kirchenbaum, H. *Values clarification: A handbook of practical strategies for teachers and students.* New York: Hart Publishing Co., 1972.

Sinauer, E. *The role of communication in international training and education: Overcoming barriers to understanding with the developing countries.* New York: Praeger, 1967.

Smith, E. Good-will tutor. *Leatherneck Magazine,* January, 1961.

Smith, M., Fawcett, J., Ezekiel, R., and Roth, S. A factorial study of morals among peace corps teachers in Ghana. *The Journal of Social Issues,* 1963, *14,* 10–32.

Sommer, R. *Personal space.* New York: Prentice-Hall, 1969.

Spector, P. An ideological weapons system. *In Conference on Research in Cross-Cultural Interaction.* Sponsored by ONR and Chaplains Corps Planning Group, 1968, 129–154.

Spector, R. Troop-community training. NATO Conference on *Special Training for Multilateral Forces.* Brussels, July, 1969.

Spector, P., Parris, T., Humphrey, R., Aronson, J., and Williams, C. Troop-community relations research in Korea, Washington, D.C., American Institutes for Research, Technical Report, April, 1969.

Spindler, G. Psychocultural adaptation. In E. Norbeck et al., Eds. *The Study of personality: an interdisciplinary appraisal.* New York: Holt, 1968, pp. 326–347.

Stein, M. Typologies in a transactional approach to assessment. Paper presented at the conference, Peace Corps and the Behavioral Sciences, Washington, D.C., 1963.

Stein, M. Creativity. In E. Borgatta, and W. Lambert, Eds. *Handbook of personality theory and research.* Chicago: Rand-McNally, 1968, 900–942.

Stewart, E. The simulation of cultural differences. *Journal of Communication,* 1966, *16,* 291–304.

Stewart, E. Simulation exercises in area training. HumRRO Professional paper 39–67 AD 660012, September, 1967(a).

Stewart, E. The simulation of cross-cultural communication. HumRRO Professional paper 50–67 AD 665053, December, 1967b.

Stewart, E., Danielian, J., and Foster, R. Simulating intercultural communication through role playing. HumRRO Technical Report 69–7, May, 1969.

Stewart, E., and Pryle, J. An approach to cultural self-awareness. HumRRO, 1966.

Stewart, E., and Rhinesmith, S. Report to the Medical Mission Sisters of overseas research on the cultural orientation program experiment. University of Delaware, Intercultural Communication, 1969.

Szanton, D. L. Cultural confrontation in the Philippines. In R. Textor, Ed. *Cultural frontiers of the Peace Corps.* Cambridge: MIT Press, 1966, 35–61.

Taba, H. *Cultural attitudes and international understanding.* New York: Institute of International Education, 1953.

Thomson, C., and English, J. The premature return of Peace Corps Volunteers. Paper presented at the conference, Peace Corps and the Behavior Sciences, Washington, D.C., 1963.

Thomson, C., and English, J. Premature return of Peace Corps Volunteers. *Public Health Reports,* 1964, *79,* 1065–1073.

Torrey, E. F. The irrelevance of traditional mental health services for urban Mexican Americans. Paper presented at the Meeting of the American Orthopsychiatric Association, 1970.

Torrey, E. F. *The mind game: witchdoctors and psychotherapists.* New York: Emerson Hall, 1971.

Torrey, E., van Rheeman, F., and Katchadourian, H. Problems of foreign students: An overview. *Journal of the American College Health Association,* December, 1970, 19.

Trail, T. F. *Education of development technicians: A guide to training programs.* New York: Praeger, 1966.

Trail, T. *Education of development technicians: A guide to training programs.* New York: Praeger, 1968.

Triandis, H. C. Interpersonal relations in international organizations. *Organizational Behavior and Human Performance,* 1967, 26–55.

Triandis, H. An analysis of cross-cultural interaction and its implications for training. In Conference on research in cross-cultural interaction, sponsored by ONR and Chaplain Corps Planning Group, 1968.

Triandis, H. C. The perception of interpersonal disagreements between supervisors and subordinates. Paper presented at NATO Symposium on Leadership and Management Appraisals. Brussels, Belgium, August, 1971.

Triandis, H. *The analysis of subjective culture.* New York: Wiley, 1972.

Triandis, H. Culture training, cognitive complexity and interpersonal attitudes. In D. Hoopes, Ed. *Readings in intercultural communication vol. III.* Pittsburgh: Intercultural communications network of the regional council for international education, 1973, pp. 55–69.

Triandis, H. Culture training, cognitive complexity and interpersonal attitudes. In R. Brislin, S. Bochner, and W. Lonner, Eds. *Cross-cultural perspectives on learning.* New York: Wiley/-Halsted, 1975, pp. 39–77.

Trifonovitch, G. On cross-cultural orientation techniques. *Topics in Culture Learning,* 1973, *1,* 38–47.

Tyler, L., Personal communication. Brigham Young University Provo, Utah: Language Research Center, 1975.

Useem, J., and Useem, R. *The western-educated man in India.* New York: Dryden Press, 1955.

Useem, J., and Useem, R. American-educated Indians and Americans in India: A comparison of two modernizing roles. *Journal of Social Issues,* 1968, *24*(4), 143–158.

Useem, J., Useem, R., and Donoghu, J. Men in the middle of the fluid culture: The role of American and non-western people in cross-cultural administration. *Human Organization,* 1963, *22* (3).

Vassiliou, V., Triandis, H., and Oncken, G. Intercultural attitudes after reading an ethnographic essay: An exploratory study. University of Illinois, Group Effectiveness Research Laboratory, Technical Report, *68* (68–13), 1968.

Vontress, C. Cultural barriers in the counseling relationship. *Personnel and Guidance Journal,* 1969, *48,* 11–17.

Vroom, V. *Work and motivation.* New York: Wiley, 1964.

Waters, S. R. The American tourist. *The Annals of the American Academy of Political and Social Science,* 1966, *368,* 109–118.

Wedge, B. Training for leadership in cross-cultural dialogue: The DATA model. In *Conference on Research in Cross-Cultural Interaction,* sponsored by ONR and Chaplain Corps Planning Group, 1968.

Weeks, W., Brislin, R., and Pedersen, P. Cross cultural units and structures for training. Honolulu: East-West Cultural Center, Culture Learning Institute, 1975.

White, R. Three not-so-obvious contributions of psychology to peace. *Journal of Social Issues,* 1969, *25*(4), 23–39.

Wicker, A. Attitudes versus actions: The relationship of verbal and overt behavioral responses to attitude objects. *Journal of Social Issues,* 1969, *25*(4), 41–78.

Wight, A. (Project Director). *Cross-cultural training: A draft handbook.* Estes Park, Colorado: Center for Research and Education, 1969.

Wilder, P. S. Overcoming barriers to educational and cultural communication. Paper presented at the meeting of the National Association for Foreign Student Affairs, Philadelphia, April–May, 1965.

Williams, R. L. Black pride, academic relevance and individual achievement. *The Counseling Psychologist,* 1970, *2*, 18–22.

Yeh, E. K., and Chu, H. M. The images of chinese and american character: Cross-cultural adaptation by chinese students. In W. Lebra, Ed. *Youth socialization and mental health.* Honolulu: East-West Center Press, 1974, pp. 200–217.

Ziffer, W. Missionary pre-service training-some observations: Part I. *International Review of Missions,* 1969, *58*(230), 195–203.

AUTHOR—SUBJECT INDEX